The Best of the Best

RICE COOKER
COOKBOOK

100
No-Fail Recipes for All Kinds of Things
That Can Be Made from Start to Finish
in Your Rice Cooker

Beth Hensperger
and Julie Kaufmann

HARVARD
COMMON
PRESS

Brimming with creative inspiration, how-to projects, and useful information to enrich your everyday life, Quarto Knows is a favorite destination for those pursuing their interests and passions. Visit our site and dig deeper with our books into your area of interest: Quarto Creates, Quarto Cooks, Quarto Homes, Quarto Lives, Quarto Drives, Quarto Explores, Quarto Gifts, or Quarto Kids.

First Published in 2019 by The Harvard Common Press, an imprint of The Quarto Group, 100 Cummings Center, Suite 265-D, Beverly, MA 01915, USA.
T (978) 282-9590 F (978) 283-2742 QuartoKnows.com

The Harvard Common Press titles are also available at discount for retail, wholesale, promotional, and bulk purchase. For details, contact the Special Sales Manager by email at specialsales@quarto.com or by mail at The Quarto Group, Attn: Special Sales Manager, 100 Cummings Center, Suite 265-D, Beverly, MA 01915, USA

23 22 21 20 19   1 2 3 4 5

ISBN: 978-1-55832-963-8

Digital edition published in 2019

The content in this book was previously published in *The Ultimate Rice Cooker* by Beth Hensperger and Julie Kaufmann (The Harvard Common Press 2012).

Design: Sporto
Food Photography: Ellen Callaway | www.CallawayPhoto.com
Food Styling: Joy Howard | joyfoodstyle.com

Printed in China

NOTE FROM THE PUBLISHER

When *The Ultimate Rice Cooker Cookbook* was first published in 2002, and then again when it appeared in an expanded and revised edition, with fifty new recipes, in 2012, it taught many thousands of home cooks how to use this inexpensive and unassuming kitchen appliance to make perfect rice of every kind, from jasmine, basmati, and Arborio to brown and black and white. It also offered many exciting recipes for things to make with your rice, such as sushi dishes, pilafs, and risottos. And, in what made the book so revolutionary, it revealed that rice cookers could make more than rice—with recipes for many other grains, such as barley, groats, couscous, hominy, and quinoa, and with inventive ways to cook beans, legumes, vegetables, and even custards and puddings in these machines.

In this volume you will find a curated selection of one hundred of the best recipes from this groundbreaking book, presented now with new photographs and in a new design. We hope these recipes make you love your rice cooker even more than you already do and that they help you get delectable meals on the table quickly and easily.

—The Editors of the Harvard Common Press

CONTENTS

It All Started with a Grain of Rice 7

The Rice Cooker Machine 9

RICE MADE PERFECTLY 22

SIMPLE RICES AND SMALL MEALS 57

PILAFS 72

RISOTTOS 86

SUSHI 93

WHOLE-GRAIN COOKING 106

POLENTA, GRITS, AND HOMINY 119

HOT CEREALS 126

BEANS, LEGUMES, AND VEGETABLES 136

WHOLE-MEAL STEAMING 150

PUDDINGS, CUSTARDS, AND FRUIT DESSERTS 159

Index 172

IT ALL STARTED
with a GRAIN of RICE

Once upon a time, rice was just rice. You planned a meal and rice seemed to be the right starch to serve with it. You placed the saucepan on the stove, measured some water into it, pulled down the bag of rice, measured it into the cup, and poured it into the boiling water. As the water came back to a boil, on went the cover and, when the timer beeped, you ate the rice.

That was before we met the rice cooker. Since then, the world of rice—the amazing array of rice available on every supermarket and specialty grocery shelf, where it grows, its lore and history, sharing recipes, the writing of this book—has become an everyday part of our lives.

To an American cook, the electric rice cooker has been, up to now, a take-it-or-leave-it kitchen appliance. But to cooks throughout Asia and many Asian-American cooks, the rice cooker is an essential appliance for everyday meal preparation. Since in many Asian cultures rice is eaten three times a day, the rice cooker is always on in every home. There are even small ones with a handle to carry while traveling on vacation or a business trip. Why eat less-than-perfect rice when you don't have to? The rice cooker is also the method of choice for cooking rice in Asian restaurants (most of the rice cooker manufacturers have a commercial division).

Rice cookers appeal to a busy cook for a number of reasons. It is an appliance well suited to a small cooking space (it is the cooking tool of choice in college dorms and is great up at the ski cabin) and boasts easy cleanup. It is a closed-environment, slow-cook method, a kind of cross between a countertop slow cooker, an oven clay pot, and a stove-top saucepan. Since it is a one-button technology, there is virtually no maintenance.

When the first edition of this book came out, not much had been written about rice cookers, beyond the slim pamphlets that come with the appliance. This book filled and continues to fill that gap, with information on how to use your rice cooker to make foolproof everyday basic rice, as well as recipes for the new rices on the market and a wealth of rice side dishes. But there is so much more: risottos and hot breakfast cereals, grains, main courses, even desserts made start to finish in your rice cooker. All instructions are presented as simply, but also as comprehensively, as possible, to be of practical use in every type and size of machine.

Your rice cooker is a versatile, convenient kitchen appliance that embraces a style of cooking that emphasizes health and natural ingredients. Rices from around the world, every one available on the market today, are covered in depth—where they come from, how to cook them, and ways to incorporate them into your meals.

THE RICE COOKER MACHINE

Congratulations on your purchase of a rice cooker. It's versatile and reliable, a very nifty little bit of technology. It can make perfect rice and, as you are about to find out, much more. The electric rice cooker is a kitchen appliance that was born in the climate of postwar Japan. Available since the early 1950s, the rice cooker is a contemporary of the electric blender, part of the surge for faster, more convenient food preparation.

At its simplest, the rice cooker machine is a removable aluminum bowl that sits atop a metal heating element within a round, insulated housing. The heating element looks like a solid metal spring the size of a quarter. It automatically can "sense" when the water is boiled off by the temperature inside the pot (the amount of water added determines the length of the cooking time, not the amount of rice) and automatically shuts the unit off. It has a round metal or glass lid with a knob handle. The bowl has a rim or handles for lifting it in and out of the appliance housing. There is a switch to push down for turning on the appliance. The switch pops up when the machine turns off. Today's models are remarkably similar in style to those first ones made by the major Japanese companies still in business today: Hitachi, Zojirushi, Sanyo, Toshiba, and Panasonic/National. Newcomers include Aroma, Rival, Cuisinart, DuPont, Krups, and many others.

The shape of the rice cooker bowl was designed to mimic the shape of the *okama*, the traditional Japanese metal pot used for cooking rice, which has a curved bottom. The slightly curved bottom is an efficient heat conductor and enables food to be cooked using the least amount of fuel. The okama was used for many centuries over an open fire or on top of a wood-burning stove. With the gradual modernization of Japanese homes, housewives adopted the electric rice cooker as a simple alternative to using up the limited space on their new electric or gas stoves. Half a century later, the electric rice cooker is a commonplace appliance in every Japanese home.

Types of Rice Cookers

There are two basic categories of rice cookers available on the market today: on/off and fuzzy logic. Within these categories there are six types of machines: cook-and-shut-off, cook-and-reduce-heat, deluxe electronic, basic fuzzy logic, and fuzzy logic combined with induction heating and/or pressure cooking. These range from simple to sophisticated, each reflecting a step in the evolution of the rice cooker. You can recognize the types not only by the range of features, but by the price, which ranges from $15 to several hundred dollars.

Choose your rice cooker by first analyzing what type of cooking you want to do with it. If you make only white rice and steam a few vegetables, go for a simpler machine. If you want the full range of timing and cooking capabilities, from porridge to brown rice, go for a more elaborate model. Models are labeled for what the cooker will do, such as Rice Cooker/Warmer or Rice Cooker/Steamer/Warmer. If you do a lot of steaming or make multi-component steamed meals, look for a model with a large steamer tray or a set of baskets; this feature is not included in fuzzy logic cookers. We are not going to recommend any particular models since technology is constantly being updated and model numbers change often. Just stay with one of the reliable brands and shop for the features you desire.

Rice cookers come in standard sizes: the 3- or 4-cup (700 or 946 ml) capacity (small), 5- or 6-cup (1.2 or 1.4 L) capacity (medium), and 8- or 10- or 14-cup (1.9 or 2.4 or 3.3 L) capacity (large) models. Many manufacturers have models that can hold up to 20 cups (4.7 L) for home use. The jumbo rice cooker, or deluxe cooker, has a capacity of 15 to 30 cups (3.5 to 7.0 L). This is a cook-and-reduce-heat machine that is great for large families, entertaining, and small cottage businesses. It is available in restaurant supply stores or online.

Look for safety features such as thermal fuse protection and an automatic cord reel. All models come with a 6-ounce (175 ml) measuring cup (see Measuring Up, page 17) and handy heat-resistant plastic rice paddle. Many come with a small steaming plate insert. If the model is designed to be portable, there will be a conveniently designed carrying handle.

ON/OFF RICE COOKERS

The two most basic types of rice cookers are the cook-and-shut-off cooker and the cook-and-reduce-heat cooker/warmer. Each has a round metal housing with a removable aluminum rice bowl. The carrying handles are on the outer housing, and there is a switch on the front of the machine. This on/off mechanism, while seemingly simple compared to the newer fuzzy logic machines, contains the same type of efficient heating elements without the digital options. In addition to making rice, it is a superior machine for steaming purposes. The cook-and-reduce heat cooker/warmer models can keep rice hot and ready to eat for several hours. The third type of on/off rice cooker is the deluxe electronic model, which is fitted with an electronic sensor unit and retains the round housing style of the other on/off cookers. These often have colorful outer housings.

Some manufacturers also have a model called the Persian-style rice cooker, designed specifically for making *chelo,* the slow-cooked Middle Eastern daily rice preparations that create their own bottom crust.

Cook-and-shut-off rice cooker. The cook-and-shut-off cooker, marketed simply as a rice cooker, is fast and safe. You push down the switch and the machine turns on. It automatically shuts off when the rice is done (when the water boils off or if the pot is removed). If you are nearby, you will hear the switch pop up.

This machine is the most basic (it is designed to make only white rice, although it does a credible job with brown rice, too, if you follow our instructions) and is very inexpensive. It is fitted with a plain aluminum cooking pot and a tempered glass or metal lid. There is no indicator light to tell you when the rice is done; if you don't hear the click as it shuts itself off, you can tell by examining the position of the switch. This is the only model that comes in a mini-size of 1 cup, for the single rice eater.

Cook-and-reduce-heat rice cooker. This rice cooker (also known as the keep warm cooker) automatically adjusts the heating element to very low heat when the thermostat senses that the water has boiled off and the rice is done. The two heat settings are On/Off and Keep Warm. This type of machine will keep rice warm for up to four hours before forming a thick crust on the bottom of the pan. There is an indicator light to let you know if the cooker is cooking or in Keep Warm mode. To turn off this rice cooker, you must unplug it.

Top-of-the-line models designed for steaming have one or two clear plastic steaming baskets with slatted tiers, which imitate the Chinese bamboo steamer baskets; this is a wonderful option. There is a tight-fitting, see-through tempered glass lid, essential to successful steaming. Less expensive models are fitted with plain aluminum cooking pots and metal lids, while the more expensive (but still comparatively inexpensive) ones have a Teflon or other nonstick rice bowl coating and glass lid. This machine usually comes with a perforated metal steamer tray that fits into the top of the rice bowl, allowing for other foods to be steamed as the rice is cooking. The cheaper models have a small tray that fits into the bottom of the bowl so that steaming is done only an inch (2.5 cm) above the element. These are very reasonably priced machines (models sell for $20 to $75), making them a great deal and a good first machine.

Deluxe electronic rice cooker. The electronic machine, designed in the 1980s, was the first big jump in rice cooker technology after its initial introduction—it cooks and keeps rice warm and moist for up to 12 hours. The temperature is controlled by a thermal-read switch. This is the type of cooker to get if you want to hold large quantities of rice for extended periods. The heating elements are located not only on the bottom, but on the sides as well, so the rice stays an even consistency and you won't get a thick crust or dry spots on the bottom of the pan. These machines are great if your family eats lots of rice and they do it at different times (for instance, if you want to make rice once a day and eat it all day long, as is done in many Asian households). You lift the lid, scoop some rice, replace the lid, and walk away, knowing that the next person will have access to warm, moist rice. There is an indicator light to let you know if the cooker is cooking or on the Keep Warm cycle.

These machines do a great job and usually come with a Teflon-coated rice bowl. Many of the deluxe electronic machines are portable.

FUZZY LOGIC RICE COOKERS

Fuzzy logic rice cookers—the basic fuzzy logic and the newer induction heating and pressure cooking machines—are immediately recognizable by their digital face, multiple-choice function buttons, and elongated housing shape, which Beth has dubbed "Queen Mum's Hatbox." These machines are not usually set up for steaming (you could use an expandable steamer basket, but it might scratch the bowl lining).

Basic fuzzy logic rice cooker. This cooker (also called the neuro fuzzy or "micom," short for microcomputerized), which hit the market in the early 1990s, is the next step up from the electronic models. Fuzzy logic technology enables the rice cooker to judge and calculate the amount of rice by weight, automatically adjusting the cooking time. Fuzzy logic rice cookers are very popular in the Asian-American food community and for good reason: They make fantastic rice. If you can afford the price and eat rice regularly, this is the machine to invest in. The first ones on the market were designed to handle white rice, especially the medium- and short-grain white rice preferred in Japan. They have evolved to incorporate multiple menus and choice of texture you prefer your rice to have (soft or hard). There are various settings, like the Quick Cook cycle (reduces the cooking time by 20 minutes), the Brown Rice cycle, and the gentle Porridge cycle. The cooking process includes brief soaking at the beginning (except when using the Quick Cook cycle) and steaming at the end. The digital 24-hour clock with timer brings freedom to the cooking process, so you can program the time you want the rice to start or finish cooking. Place the ingredients in the pot, set the timer, and the rice or meal is ready when you are. After the food is cooked, the unit automatically switches to the Keep Warm cycle, which keeps foods moister than in conventional models, up to 12 hours. These machines come with non-stick bowls so easy to clean you will wish every pan you own was just like it.

Find these machines in Asian markets (larger Asian supermarkets will stock a variety of models) or through major online retailers such as Target and Amazon, as well as kitchenware retailers such as Sur la Table and Williams-Sonoma.

Here we want to make note of a special fuzzy logic rice cooker—one with a natural clay bowl instead of a metal one. The VitaClay is the brainchild of Michelle Liu, a former Silicon Valley computer hardware engineer who dreamed of going into business for herself. We find the Vita-Clay makes great tasting rice. The clay pot and its matching lid clean easily with a sponge and soapy water. It's available in both 6- and 8-cup (1.4 and 1.9 L) sizes, and in electronic as well as fuzzy-logic models. The VitaClay is sold online through major retailers as well as directly from www.vitaclay-chef.com.

Fuzzy logic rice cooker with induction heating. The induction heating cooker uses magnetic principles to create heat throughout the pan, not just at the bottom, resulting in a finished product that is more evenly cooked.

These are expensive machines, though the price is coming down.

Fuzzy logic rice cooker with pressure cooking. As devotees of the stovetop pressure cooker have known for years, brown rice cooks up especially well under pressure—light, fluffy—and faster than other conventional methods. The new upscale fuzzy-logic pressure rice cookers are expensive but winning rave reviews.

How the Rice Cooker Works (The Scientific Scoop)

The best rice cooker rice is achieved by the following steps: washing or rinsing, soaking, boiling, and steaming. It is a variation of stovetop cooking, a boil-steam method known as the Canton style.

TIPS FOR BUYING A RICE COOKER ABROAD

If you are traveling to or through many of the major airports in Asia, you'll find a large selection of high-end rice cookers in the duty-free electronics shops. Julie's beloved Sanyo fuzzy logic rice cooker came from the Tokyo airport. At the time, there were about 15 rice cookers to choose from, priced from $80 to more than $400 for the large fuzzy logic models. Obviously these are not the under-$20 models found in many American variety stores, but serious machines for serious cooks.

Important Note: Before you buy abroad, double-check to make sure the machine runs on U.S. current, has a U.S.-style plug, and comes with English-language instructions and English-language buttons (Julie's is labeled in English and Chinese). Generally speaking, if you're visiting Asia, you'll be better off shopping for your rice cooker at the airport instead of in town. The airport is the best place to find rice cookers meant for the English-speaking consumer.

WASHING OR RINSING THE RICE

The washing or rinsing (depending on the type of rice) is done by hand before you place the rice in the cooker. Almost all serious consumers of rice rinse rice thoroughly before cooking, but it is purely optional. There are good reasons to do so. Cooking instructions in the U.S. instruct you not to rinse rice because, by law, rice meant for the American consumer has been fortified with powdered vitamins that will be removed if you rinse it. If you want the vitamins (which are not necessary if you have a well-balanced diet), then do not wash or rinse. If you want the best quality cooked rice, then washing removes much of the loose surface starch, which will reduce excess stickiness. The difference is subtle, but a serious real rice eater can tell the difference: The flavor is cleaner, the whiteness improves, and the rice is less sticky.

Important Note: Arborio and other risotto-style rices should never be washed before using, because the surface starch is what makes risotto creamy.

SOAKING THE RICE

Soaking rice about an hour before cooking allows moisture to get to the center of the kernel, reduces cooking time, and improves the final texture. During the boiling phase, the heat will transfer more quickly to the center and the rice will be done six to eight minutes faster, causing the least amount of damage to the outside of the delicate kernels. Soaking can be done outside the cooker, or in the rice cooker bowl with the cover closed before turning on the machine. In fuzzy logic machines, a short soak period is automatically timed in all but the Quick Cook cycle.

BOILING THE RICE

Rice needs to cook in hot water in order to for moisture to penetrate the grains and transfer the heat necessary to gelatinize the starch in rice. When you turn on your rice cooker, it begins to slowly heat the contents of the rice bowl. Soon the water boils and the grains of rice begin absorbing water; you will hear the rice and water start to bubble in the machine. (In fuzzy logic rice cookers, there is a built-in soak cycle for the rice, designed to help it absorb water better. In that case, it may appear to take a long time for the water to boil. Don't worry. When the time is right, the cooker will kick into high gear and boil the water.)

It takes about 15 minutes in boiling water for moisture and heat to penetrate to the center of the rice kernel. If you look inside the cooker during this period, you will see semi-cooked rice with steam holes over the surface. These are caused by pockets of water vapor that formed on the pan bottom and have risen to the surface. The water bubbles in the cooker until the temperature exceeds 212°F (100°C) and then the cooker shuts off. The temperature of water cannot exceed 212°F (100°C), so the cooker knows all the water is gone when the temperature hits a few degrees higher. (This is the secret to how the cooker knows the rice is ready.) Do not remove the cover at this time.

STEAMING THE RICE

In the new on/off and fuzzy logic cookers, the steaming period is built into the regular cooking cycle, and the Keep Warm cycle is an extended low-heat steaming period. In simpler models, you set a timer or note the time. The rice cooker switches from the cooking cycle to the Keep Warm cycle (or, in simple on/off machines, simply shuts off). But your rice isn't finished yet. Now is when the steaming process takes place.

Steaming is a key part of the cooking process. It allows further cooking of the rice without any swelling damage to the starch inside the grain. Ten minutes of steaming is adequate for most models of rice cooker and most rices; if your rice still seems wet at the end of 10 minutes, cover the cooker, and check at 5-minute intervals. Once the rice has properly steamed, uncover the rice cooker and stir or fluff the rice thoroughly but gently with a wooden or plastic rice paddle or wooden spoon. Replace the cover if you are not serving the rice immediately. Rice is not done until the center of each grain is completely cooked. Most rice is perfectly cooked when its moisture content is between 58 and 64 percent, though the final moisture content is a matter of preference and differs with every type of rice. Some fuzzy logic machines have a setting for regular, soft, and firm textures, varying the amount of moisture in the rice. The more water per cup of rice, the longer the machine will cook the rice.

Machines without a Keep Warm cycle just turn off when the regular cycle is finished. You let the rice steam for the specified time after the machine shuts off. There is enough retained heat to accomplish the steaming. You can hold the rice in the machine for as long as it stays warm, certainly for an hour, but the exact time depends on the machine, its size, and how full it is. This is a place where you have to use your judgment.

THE FACE OF THE RICE COOKER

On the front of each rice cooker body is the cooking control panel. There are three distinctly different faces to the multitude of rice cookers: One is the simple on/off machine, which has a manual cooking indicator switch and prominent power indicator light; the second is the simple digital readout and indicator lights found on the deluxe electronic models. These may look different but the basic functions are the same as for the on/off cookers: Cook and Keep Warm. Finally, there is the more complex digital face of the fuzzy logic cookers, which has a clock and buttons for various cooking cycles and choices. Here is a simplified guide to all these controls. As always, carefully read your manufacturer's manual to familiarize yourself with your particular machine.

ON/OFF AND DELUXE ELECTRONIC COOKERS

The on/off cookers have a switch that can be clicked into an up or down position—down being the On or Cook cycle and up being the Off or Keep Warm cycle. Both positions snap securely into place. Cook and Keep Warm both deliver a constant heat, although at two different temperatures: On is the high temperature and Keep Warm is the low temperature.

The power indicator light is lit as soon as the machine is plugged in, and the machine immediately heats up depending on which position the switch is in. There may be a secondary indicator light labeled Cook or Keep Warm, the easy visual for identifying immediately where the switch is set. The Cook position equates to the regular cycle in the fuzzy logic machines. To cook rice, you must press the switch down to Cook; when the cooker senses the rice is done, it will automatically snap to the up, or Keep Warm, position. It will hold the Keep Warm position until you unplug the machine (which you must do to turn it off). Note that

the least expensive cookers do not have a Keep Warm feature.

Deluxe electronic cookers may have digital controls but function in essentially the same way. Some have a clock and timer for time-delayed cooking.

FUZZY LOGIC AND OTHER ADVANCED COOKERS

The digital control panel, manipulated with buttons (also referred to as keys), will vary slightly from brand to brand, but they all have basically the same features. You will have a main Cooking/Reheat button, and one for Keep Warm (which can be used to reset the program by stopping the cycle at any point). You may have a button for an Extended Keep Warm cycle on models in which the regular Keep Warm is designed for only the first three hours after rice is made. The Timer button can be used to trigger the memory capabilities of the machine and preset the timer for starting the machine automatically. Refer to your manufacturer's manual for the specific steps for setting the timer. Remember that your rice will be soaking while waiting for the machine to turn on. To prevent spoilage, never leave rice soaking in a meat or poultry broth or with perishable ingredients.

All the buttons/keys have their own indicator lamp to visually cue you where the machine is in the cycle. Only one indicator lamp will be lit at a time. It may feel awkward the first few times you program the cooker, but you'll get the hang of it quickly.

KEEP WARM CYCLE

When the rice is done, both on/off and fuzzy logic machines will automatically switch to the constant low (but hot enough for serving) temperature of the Keep Warm mode. On fuzzy logic machines, there may be a digital readout in hours of how long the rice has been held on Keep Warm. In machines with a two-cycle Keep

Warm function, the Keep Warm cycle will automatically shut off after three hours, or you can stop the machine by pressing the button (the light will go out). In these machines, the light for the Keep Warm cycle goes out at the end of the time period, the Extended Keep Warm clicks in, and an even lower temperature will take over for an additional eight hours (we don't recommend serving the rice at this temperature). In some machines, at the end of the eight hours, the machine will automatically switch back to the Keep Warm cycle. You can press Extended Keep Warm at any time or press Keep Warm to heat the rice back up to a serving temperature. In on/off machines, the Keep Warm stays on until you unplug the machine.

These cycles are based on cooking medium-grain white rice. Be sure to refer to specific recipes for the recommended amount of time to safely hold various types of rice and more complex rice preparations on Keep Warm. Even white rice will dry out or spoil when left for extended periods on Keep Warm. Dishes that include any type of meat, fish, beans, or vegetables should always be eaten as soon as possible after the cooking cycle is completed to avoid spoilage. Brown rice can sour when left on Keep Warm for more than an hour (especially in hot weather), and glutinous rice loses its desirable texture. The Keep Warm cycle also automatically clicks in after the Porridge cycle (see below and page 10) has completed, but rice porridge, such as congee, should not be left on Keep Warm.

MENU

The Menu button is the first button you will press to make your choices for how your machine will cook your rice. It is automatically set for a white rice cycle. You select the desired texture (Regular—sometimes called Normal—Softer, Harder, Porridge, Quick Cook), and an audio signal will beep and a visual indicator signal will rotate counterclockwise through these positions as you press the button. The white rice button is sometimes labeled White/Brown, but some machines have separate settings for both brown rice and sushi rice, which need to be cooked to textures very different than regular white rice.

- **Regular/Softer/Harder.** The machine is automatically set for Regular (or Normal) when first plugged in. If you want something other than that, you will use the Menu button to set it. Regular is usually the setting for cooking white rice, brown rice, mixed rice, and glutinous rice. Select the Softer setting if you like your white rice a softer consistency. Select the Harder setting for rice to be used in rice salads and preparations such as stuffing where the rice will be further cooked with other ingredients.

- **Quick Cook cycle.** Some fuzzy logic rice cookers have a Quick Cook cycle as well as a Regular cycle. The Quick Cook cycle bypasses the Regular cycle's built-in soak time and is convenient when you want rice in a hurry. It is also handy in one other situation: when you are sautéing ingredients in the rice cooker bowl. When you are finished sautéing and are ready to add the liquid and proceed with the recipe, you can cancel the Quick Cook cycle and program whatever cycle is required for the recipe, or, if the recipe does not require an alternate cycle, simply let the Quick Cook cycle complete. In the Quick Cook mode, you cannot select the texture of the rice.

- **Porridge cycle.** Fuzzy logic machines all offer a Porridge cycle, which is designed to cook the rice breakfast porridge enjoyed throughout Asia. It has a medium-low, constant set temperature different than for the regular cycle and the Keep Warm cycle. On/off machines do not have this feature.

  In our testing, we were pleasantly surprised to find that the gentle heat of the

45-minute Porridge cycle works well for preparing risotto, mushes like polenta, grits, and hominy, as well as hot breakfast cereals. It also makes knockout applesauce and is a great vehicle for poaching fruit.

The Porridge cycle can be set for a second time to extend cooking time when necessary. This eliminates the need to use the automatic timer. If you need only a portion of the cycle, set a kitchen timer and then cancel the program. The cooking process will stop immediately and you can serve your dish.

One additional note about the Porridge cycle: We have had great success in certain rice cookers with milk-based desserts such as tapioca and rice puddings made using the Porridge cycle. However, some rice cookers' Porridge cycles can't handle milk (and this varies from individual machine to individual machine), and you will be cleaning up a messy boilover if you try. If you want to try these recipes in your rice cooker, stay nearby the first time you do it and be prepared to turn off the machine if the milk looks like it's going to boil over.

- **GABA cycle.** Some of the newest, most advanced induction style rice cookers have a special cycle for preparing GABA, or germinated or sprouted brown rice. GABA stands for gamma-aminobutyric acid. The GABA cycle provides a two-hour soak in warm water before cooking. Note that if you purchase germinated brown rice at the store, the rice has already been soaked (for longer than two hours, by the way) and dried before packaging, and it is ready to cook in any rice cooker according to the instructions on page 51.

- **Reheat.** Some fuzzy logic machines have a Reheat mode. The Reheat mode is on the same button as the main button for turning on the machine, labeled Cooking. It can be used to bring rice that has been kept on the Keep Warm cycle, or leftover or refrigerated rice, back up to a hot serving temperature. (On machines without this feature, Keep Warm is serving temperature.) The machine will beep as soon as the right temperature is reached, usually about 5 to 10 minutes, then switch automatically to the Keep Warm cycle. Most rice on Reheat, especially cold rice, needs a tablespoon or two (15 to 28 ml) of water per cup (235 ml) drizzled over it to rehydrate properly to a soft consistency. We recommend that you eat the rice as soon as the Reheat cycle indicates it is done rather than leave it on Keep Warm (possibly for a second time) for the best consistency and to prevent a tough bottom layer from forming.

Rice Cooker Basics

Here are a few tips and basic pieces of information that will help you get the most from your rice cooker.

Our first bit of advice is to carefully review the manufacturer's booklet that comes with your rice cooker. Brands do differ. Orient yourself to the parts of the machine and the list of safety precautions.

MEASURING UP

Measuring the rice correctly is of crucial importance for success in your rice cooker. Please read this section carefully before making your first pot of rice. Please note that the recipes in this book are designed to use a standard U.S. measure for both solid and liquid ingredients (water and broth), as well as measuring spoons for spices and flavor enhancers.

- Don't throw away the little plastic measuring cup that comes with your rice cooker. That measuring cup is the standard unit of measurement for your machine, although you can use the U.S. standard measure if you choose. You just need to be consistent. However, be aware that when the booklet that came with your rice cooker says to put in 2 cups of rice and add water to the "2-cup" level on the bowl, that means you are supposed to measure the rice with that little cup, not with one of your regular measuring cups. This is very important if you make recipes from the booklet. A rice cooker cup holds 180 milliliters (about 6 ounces or ¾ of a U.S. cup) and a standard U.S. cup holds 235 milliliters, so there is a significant difference. Throughout this book, we will refer to this unit of measurement as a "rice cooker cup."

- In this book, our recipes, even the Asian-style ones and the measurement charts for plain rice, use a standard 8-ounce (235 ml) measuring cup form of measurement. If we use the rice cooker cup instead of the standard measure, we always specify the difference. But even when we measure rice with the rice cooker cup, we measure liquids using the U.S. standard cups. Why? We've found it most convenient to keep our rice cooker cups clean, dry, and ready to use with rice and other grains. It's also difficult to measure liquids (especially larger quantities) precisely with the little cups.

- Rice cooker directions are beginning to appear on the back of packages of rice, especially on brands that are marketed to Asian-American consumers. Usually, the directions are given in rice cooker cups, even if the directions just say "cups." This is frequently also the case for rice cooker recipes that you find on the Internet. Unfortunately, it can be difficult to know the difference.

- If a friend shares a rice cooker recipe with you, it's a good idea to ask, in the case of both solid and liquid ingredients, "Is this in rice cooker cups or regular U.S. cups?"

MAKING THAT FIRST POT OF RICE IN YOUR RICE COOKER

1. Measure the desired amount of rice. Don't mound the rice in the measuring cup—level it off with a sweep of your finger or a table knife. For reference, 1 pound (455 g) of raw rice is equal to a bit more than 3 rice cooker cups.

2. Some cooks swear by coating the rice cooker

bowl with a film of nonstick cooking spray or 1 teaspoon of vegetable oil to prevent sticking and to keep the rice grains a bit more separate (especially brown rice). While some of our recipes call for this step, it is optional.

3. If desired, rinse or wash the rice, or follow the instructions in each specific recipe for any presoaking, depending on the type of rice. Many cooks wash the rice right in the rice cooker bowl, even though the instructions that come with many machines say not to. (If you choose to do this, and we frequently do, we promise not to tell.)

4. Place the drained rice in the bowl of your rice cooker; if the rice is wet, you may need a rubber spatula to get all of the grains out of the rinsing bowl. Place the bowl into the body of the rice cooker machine. With your hand or a rice spatula, spread out the rice into a fairly flat layer over the entire bottom surface of the bowl. This helps it cook evenly.

5. Measure and add the required amount of cold liquid to the bowl. Use bottled or filtered water rather than tap water for the best tasting rice. You can use the lines on the inside of the rice cooker bowl as a guide. If you have put in 1 rice cooker cup of rice, add water to the "1" line. More elaborate rice cookers (especially the fuzzy logic models) often have several sets of lines on the bowl, indicating the amount of water needed for regular rice, "soft" rice, "hard" rice, brown rice, sushi rice, or rice porridge. Follow the correct line for the type of rice you are making. If you choose to measure the rice in U.S. dry measuring cups, the lines on the bowl will not apply. You will add liquid measured in a U.S. measuring cup according to the recipe you have selected.

6. Many people, especially those raised in Asian households, swear by the finger-measuring method. Plop in the desired amount of rice, smooth it out, and add water until the level comes to the first knuckle on your index finger, with your fingertip just touching the surface of the rice. Many experienced rice cooks measure in this manner, a relatively constant level of water above the level of the rice (about ½ inch [1.3 cm]), regardless of the quantity of rice.

7. Some people like their rice a little bit softer; some, a little bit harder. As you become an experienced rice cooker owner, you will develop your own preferences. If you want softer rice, you'll add a bit more water; for firmer rice, you'll add a bit less.

8. Add salt, if called for in the recipe, give the mixture a swirl with your finger or a rice paddle, and close the cover.

9. Plug in the unit and arrange the cooker on your counter away from the wall and out from under the cabinets so the steam can escape the vent without hindrance.

10. On fuzzy logic machines, choose the regular White Rice/Brown Rice cycle, then press Cooking/Cook. On the cook-and-keep-warm or cook-and-shut-off machines, simply press down on the switch. No peeking, please! The hot steam inside the machine is what is cooking the rice; open the cover and the moisture is lost as the steam evaporates, and the moderate pressure and heat that have naturally built up will dissipate in an instant cloud. The rice cooker uses the same principles and process of cooking as a covered pot on the stove: You boil the mixture until all of the water is evaporated or absorbed. The main advantage of

a rice cooker is that it knows when to stop cooking automatically, thanks to a sensitive built-in thermostat, and prevents the scorching normally associated with stovetop methods.

11. The steaming period at the end of the cooking cycle is crucial to your success. It is the time when the rice "rests" and any extra liquid is absorbed. In fuzzy logic cookers, this period is often automatically programmed in. When the finish "beep" sounds, the rice is really done, steaming and all. In on/off cookers, you must listen for the "click" when the machine switches off the cooking cycle and into the Keep Warm cycle. (In very inexpensive on/off cookers, there is no Keep Warm mode.

A NOTE ABOUT MACHINE SIZES

In addition to information about machine type, each recipe is labeled with a size of rice cooker: small (4-cup), medium (6-cup [1.4 L]), or large (10-cup). The size given is the one that works best for the recipe. In many cases, though, you can adjust the recipe for a smaller or larger rice cooker by increasing or decreasing ingredients. However, do not exceed the manufacturer's stated capacity for your machine.

Let the rice rest, covered, for the specified time in the machine; set a timer or note the time on a piece of paper.) For the best textured rice, let the cooked rice rest 10 to 15 minutes after the cooking cycle has ended with a small or medium rice cooker, 15 to 20 minutes with a large one. This gives the rice time to settle and absorb a bit more moisture, softening the starch a bit further.

12. When the "resting" period is over, open the cooker cover and stir the rice thoroughly but gently with a wooden or plastic rice paddle, or a wooden spoon. If you are not ready to serve the rice, re-cover or close the lid immediately to keep it warm on the Keep Warm cycle, if your model has one.

13. Enjoy eating your perfectly cooked rice!

CLEANUP

It is recommended that any submersible parts of the rice cooker be washed by hand, not in a dishwasher. Even with cooked-on rice, a quick soak in cold water has always been all that is needed to quickly clean the bowl. The simplest machines have an uncoated aluminum bowl. If your bowl has a Teflon or SilverStone nonstick coating, use a sponge or plastic scrubber that will not scratch its surface. The machine housing needs only a sponge-down after unplugging; it should never be immersed in water.

How to Use This Book

Many of the recipes in this book can be made in either an on/off or fuzzy logic machine, but some can be prepared in only one or the other. If you are not sure what type of machine you have, refer to page 8. Before starting a recipe, please make sure you have the recommended machine for that recipe. For more on the cycles, refer to pages 14–16.

THE REGULAR CYCLE

In the recipes, the Regular cycle refers to the basic cooking program for the on/off and fuzzy logic machines. To begin the Regular cycle in the on/off machine, you press or flip the switch to the Cook position. To begin the Regular cycle in a fuzzy logic machine, simply press that button. The Quick Cook program is an abbreviated cycle of the Regular cycle on the fuzzy logic machines. The Brown Rice cycle is an extended Regular cycle with a soaking time added. It is best used for short-grain brown rices and long-cooking whole grains, such as whole buckwheat groats, farro, and wheat berries. It is exclusively a feature of the more temperature-sensitive fuzzy logic machines. The Sushi cycle is exclusively for cooking short-grain white rices, and is also an extended Regular cycle and exclusively a fuzzy logic feature, although sushi rice can be cooked on the Regular cycle.

The recipes in the chapters below can be made using the Regular cycle in both types of machines, but for the best results, check the key information at the top of the recipe regarding the machine size and Keep Warm limits.

Rice Made Perfectly, Simple Rices and small Meals; Pilafs; Whole-Grain Cooking; Sushi

THE PORRIDGE CYCLE

The Porridge cycle is an exclusive feature of the fuzzy logic machines. While we have found that many of the recipes in the chapters listed below can be made in the on/off machines using the Regular cycle (check each recipe), the results are not as satisfactory as on the Porridge cycle. This is because the on/off machines run at a higher temperature that maintains a full rolling boil and, if there is a lot of liquid in the recipe, such as for risotto, the machine will not automatically turn off. The Porridge cycle has a longer, gentle simmer. For the best results, be sure to check the key information at the top of the recipe regarding machine size to avoid boilover. And, again, do take care with milk-based puddings—these work beautifully in some machines while in others the milk boils over. The first time you try a milk-based recipe, stay near the cooker and be ready to turn it off if necessary.

Polenta, Grits, and Hominy; Hot Cereals; Puddings, Custards and Fruit Desserts

STEAMING IN THE RICE COOKER

Unless foods are placed directly on top of the rice, steaming is a feature that works best in the on/off machines. We recommend the large (10-cup) cooker fitted with a steamer plate in the bottom of the bowl, an insert tray, or a set of stacked steamer baskets for most of these recipes.

The fuzzy logic machines with their attached covers do not have the wide range of steamer capabilities of the on/off machines. For the best results, please carefully read the hints for successful steaming on pages 6 and 7 before making the recipes in the following chapters.

Beans, Legumes, and Vegetables; Whole-Meal Steaming; Dim Sum, Dolmas, and Tamales: Little Bites; Puddings, Custards, and Fruit Desserts

RICE
MADE PERFECTLY

American Long-Grain White Rice — 1

Chinese-Style Plain Rice — 2

Converted Rice — 3

American Jasmine Rice — 4

Thai Jasmine Rice — 5

Medium-Grain White Rice — 6

Japanese White Rice with Umeboshi and Sesame — 7

Riso — 8

Short-Grain White Rice — 9

Steamed Sticky Rice — 10

Long- or Medium-Grain Brown Rice — 11

Short-Grain Brown Rice — 12

Germinated Brown Rice — 13

Brown Basmati Rice — 14

Wehani Rice — 15

Black Rice — 16

Buddha is said to have existed on one grain of cooked rice per day while on his early ascetic path. His mendicant disciples are given the credit for the spread of the rice culture, along with its cooking pots, making rice basic fare throughout Southeast Asia and China. For the Buddhists, this set the atmosphere to imbue the grain with the power for supernatural nourishment (thus making rice the food of alms throughout Asia) as well as a simply wholesome foodstuff (the first food an Indian bride serves her new husband). Japanese Zen Buddhists have lent the name "little Buddha" to each grain in their rice bowls; children love the association.

The gentleman-scholar Confucius, a contemporary of Buddha, was known as the apostle of virtuous living and a gourmet. He is said to have established the philosophical basis for today's Chinese cuisine: food that combines the attributes of fine sensory aesthetics with inner harmony. His meticulously prepared daily rice bowl, always perfectly white, would be the background for the jewel-like colors of contrasting or similarly hued complementary foods, served in a bowl that was also a work of notable artistry. This is the ancestry of the rice, cooked in basically the same manner, that graces our tables today.

Rice, the most popular grain in the world, comes in a wide variety of textures, colors, sizes, and tastes. It is grown in every temperate and tropical zone on this earth. The explosion of interest in traditional ethnic cuisines, from Asian to Middle Eastern cooking, has introduced a staggering array of different types of rices to the home cook. After cooking, some rices are dry, with each grain delightfully separate, while others are moist and sticky. All types can be cooked successfully in a rice cooker. Of all existing species of rice in the plant world, only two types have been cultivated. One is native to the African continent and the other, *Oryza* sativa, is indigenous to Asia. This latter species is the rice that the world eats, knows, and loves. There have been tens of thousands of varieties, cultivated and cross-cultivated off the early ones, over a multitude of centuries.

There are two distinctly different shapes of *Oryza sativa*. One is long and slender, known as *indica*, or long-grain rice. The other is short, plump, and more translucent, known as *japonica*, or short-grain. Once you have these two types set in your mind, you have the key to knowing the basics about rice. Within each type of rice, there are many varieties. While some people think that rice is just rice, so very many traditional dishes call for a specific rice in their preparation. *Indica* (for India) is the grain of choice for pilafs, a favorite Western rice dish. It is a low-starch rice and cooks up dry, with each grain separate from the others. This is the preferred rice for salads and a pile of plain old hot rice and butter for dinner. Long-grain rice can be rather bland, like extra-long Carolina gold, or aromatic, like Thai jasmine and Indian basmati. Long-grain rice always requires more liquid to cook properly than medium- and short-grain white rices. Long-grain rices are popular in all cuisines of the Western world and are the rice of choice in India, China, and the Philippines.

Japonica (for Japan) includes short- and medium-grain rices. While Americans make a distinction between short- and medium-grain rices, please note that outside the United States these rices are both known as short-grain rice. These are the rices grown in Southeast Asia, Korea, and Japan and are generally not exported. The University of California at Davis developed the variety of medium-grain rice so beloved by Japanese-Americans, called Calrose, and a good portion of the California rice-growing land north of Sacramento is devoted to this and similar varieties of rice. The finest short- and medium-grain domestic rices are such superior rices that we were told they are brought as house gifts when visiting in Japan.

Short-grain rice is known for its clumpy, clingy nature, perfect for eating with chopsticks, and often eaten only when dining at a Japanese restaurant. It is beautifully made at home in the rice cooker, giving your sushi or Japanese recipes that wonderful authentic touch. There is also a short-grain sticky rice, sometimes known as sweet rice (it is not sugar-sweet) or glutinous rice. This is a specialty rice eaten in Japan, parts of southern China, and the mountainous northern areas of Indonesia, Thailand, and Vietnam, where it is rolled into balls and popped into the mouth. This type of rice is usually steamed, rather than boiled like other rices, because it is mercilessly sticky otherwise. It is also used in rice desserts and porridge.

Different varieties of *japonica* rice are grown in northern Italy, France, and Spain. These have plenty of the starch amylopectin and are featured in the traditional dishes of these areas, risotto and paella. Medium-grain rice is the rice of choice in the Caribbean, Central America, and Japan. Medium- and short-grain rices are nice for rice pudding, giving it a thick, naturally creamy consistency.

Rices are further categorized by how each is processed. Plain white rice, whether long-, medium-, or short-grained, is processed, or milled, by a procedure called *polishing*. The bran and germ are removed (hulled) to make the grain

more digestible and faster to cook. It is then enriched by spraying it with thiamine, which is lost when the bran is discarded. Thiamine is needed for the proper metabolizing of carbohydrates and iron.

Brown, or unhulled, rice is a whole grain, with its bran and outer layer of fiber intact. It has all the vitamins and minerals rice has to offer. Because of the oil-rich bran, it is best kept refrigerated or frozen, rather than on the cupboard shelf, where it can go rancid. Brown rice will always take at least twice the amount of time to cook as white rice.

In the United States, more and more specialty rice varieties are being grown for niche markets. Several varieties of rice have been developed to perform like the imported white Thai jasmine and Indian basmati. There are numerous varieties of rice that have unusual bran colors, like Wehani, red rice, and black rice, all technically considered brown rices.

Converted rice is long-grain white rice that has been parboiled and dried before refining. It is an excellent, firm white rice; do not confuse it with instant rice. We don't usually use Minute rice or instant rice, which is completely precooked and dehydrated. Cooking up quite mushy, instant rice just cannot compare with fresh-cooked white rice. But if you are backpacking or traveling (and cooking in your motel room), instant rice has its place.

There is a place for every type of rice in the home kitchen. No rice is better or worse than another; it is totally dependent on your own palate. "Rice is a live thing," says Ken Lee, co-owner of Lotus Foods, a specialty rice import company with its headquarters in El Cerrito, California. "You have to pay attention since every rice can vary from time to time." This accounts for the rice you make every day looking, behaving, and tasting just that little bit different, even though you made it the same way you always do. If you buy rice in bulk, note the proportions of liquid to rice that worked best for that batch and be prepared to reassess the recipe when you buy your next batch of rice. Variables include the time of year, how old the rice is, what grade you bought, and how the rice was stored; it changes all the time.

When buying or evaluating rice, you want to look at the color of the grains; they should be pearly (for white rice) or shiny (for red or black rice) or evenly tan (for brown rice). The grains should be the same size, without a lot of broken grains or milling bits in the bag (and certainly no bugs!). Judge the aroma of both the uncooked and cooked grain; every single rice will have a different fragrance, from floral, grassy, nutty, or herbaceous to earthy and musty. The aroma will blossom and intensify after cooking into a bouquet of sorts. Some rices lose their aroma as they cool. Then there is the final texture, which is dictated by the amount of water absorbed during the cooking; some people like chewy rice, others like it mushy. And, finally, judge the overall flavor of each rice. Sweet and nutty to wholesome and bland, each rice is an adventure to the palate.

Every recipe in this book will specify what type of rice is needed, so you won't have to wonder when a recipe says "rice" what it means. Keep your cupboard stocked with different rices and, before you know it, you will be a bona fide rice lover with a vast repertoire of different rices that are less than an hour away from serving.

Long-Grain Rices

The kernel of long-grain rice is slender and about four times as long as it is wide.

CAROLINA LONG-GRAIN RICE

Carolina gold, America's long-grain indica rice, was first grown in the waterlands of North and South Carolina during the eighteenth century. It is also known as southern long-grain. Dozens of varieties of this rice have been developed. This is the most common type of rice consumed in the United States—and the world—as a table rice, beloved for its dry, separate grains and bland sweet-grain flavor. After the destruction of the Civil War, growing shifted to Texas on the Gulf of Mexico, Arkansas, the Missouri riverbeds, and the Louisiana Mississippi delta, all areas with a specific type of soil and moisture perfect for rice growing, where its cultivation flourishes to this day. The top producers are Arkansas, then Texas, and the northern Central Valley of California. Some brands will have the state of origin on the bag (look at the address in the small print on the side of the bag); others will be generically labeled "long-grain rice." There are slight differences among varieties, and many varieties are kept separate for special processing like parboiling (converted rice), while similar rices are mixed and packaged under the generic label by super-companies like Uncle Ben's and Riviana (Mahatma). American long-grain rice is good for casseroles, side dishes, curries, pilafs, jambalaya, salads, chili, stuffings, and waffles.

ASIAN LONG-GRAIN RICE

Part of the royal duties of Chinese princes was to plant the first grains of rice at the beginning of each growing season. In China, rice growing has been an agricultural passion for millennia, rivaling that of India. In Mandarin, a bowl of plain rice is known as *fan*, or rice bowl rice. Asian long-grain rice is a slightly moist rice, but not sticky like Japanese medium- or short-grain, or dry and separate, like Indian basmati or converted rice. It is never aromatic. It is pure, simple rice at its most basic.

Inspect a pile of rice sacks in the corner of your Asian specialty market, labeled in Chinese, and this will be Asian-style long-grain rice. This is the rice called for in Chinese recipes, served in Chinese restaurants and for fried rice. It is the preferred rice in China, Taiwan, and parts of Southeast Asia. Little of this rice is exported, so unless you shop in Asian grocery stores, any type of Carolina rice can be substituted.

AROMATIC LONG-GRAIN RICE

Known for their authentic floral-incense scents emitted during cooking, aromatic rices are exceptionally popular now for all-around cooking purposes. They were once served to Asian royalty and reserved for religious holidays. Varieties are now being grown domestically, but connoisseurs seek out the imported brands.

Basmati rice, which translates to the "queen of fragrance," is imported from the Indian Himalayan foothills of the Ganges Valley and Pakistan. Its distinctive flavor is an integral part of the cuisine of India and is said to be the result of the combination of the Himalayan headwaters and the soil of the Punjab, the famous ancient valleys of the Indus River and its tributaries (the best grade still comes from this region). Fine basmati commands high prices. This rice has a high amylose content and a firm, almost dry texture when properly cooked. The raw kernel is long and slender like southern long-grain, but is slightly smaller, and the kernels increase in length by more than three times when cooked to produce a very long, slender cooked grain. The best Indian basmati has been aged for at least one year (with no broken grains in the bag) to increase the firmness of the cooked texture and increase the elongation achieved in cooking. It is simply one of the finest rices grown, with a rich flavor, and is perfect for pilafs, curry, *biryani*, casseroles, and sweet puddings. It is a great all-purpose rice. Excellent brands include Pari, Daawat, and Tilda, although if you shop in Indian groceries, the bags can also be labeled by the area in which the rice is grown.

Thai jasmine has a lovely muted floral quality akin to the scent of tropical flowers (hence the name) and is more nut-sweet than basmati; it is the second most popular aromatic rice in America. While classified as a long-grain rice and looking much like Carolina rice before and after cooking, it contains the same amount of moisture as medium-grain rice and cooks up more similar to that type. The national rice of Thailand, it is ever so slightly sticky and tender compared to basmati. The rice is best consumed after the new crop is harvested, as the rice hardens in texture and loses aroma with time. There are many varieties being grown in the United States in imitation of this unique type of rice, with Jasmati being the best offshoot of the lot. There is now a Texas-grown domestic organic jasmine (both white and brown) available from Lowell Farms that is a must for jasmine rice lovers. The first American-grown jasmine is marketed in cloth sacks by Della and grown in the delta areas of Arkansas and Missouri. For a lovely salad, steep a jasmine tea bag in the cooking water for a few minutes before you make a pot of jasmine rice. Jasmine is not the traditional Chinese rice, but today many Chinese-American consumers are making the switch. Good brands are Mahatma, Pacific International (formerly Homai), and Tilda, labeled *Riz Parfumé*.

Calmati, *Texmati*, *Kasmati*, and *Jasmati* are all domestic offshoots of the wonderful but more intensely flavored aromatics. Calmati is an Indian basmati crossed with regional varieties of Carolina long-grain grown in California. Texmati, a Texas long-grain basmati adapted to the area, was bred twenty years ago by RiceTec, Inc., and was the first grain in their line of hybrids. Texmati is part of RiceSelect's Royal Blend, a combination of white and brown Texmati with scarified wild rice, so that all the types cook in the same amount of time. Kasmati rice has a stronger aroma and firmer center of the grain, which is visible upon inspecting the individual grains. These three rices have basmati's viscosity and cooking style, but smaller individual grains. Jasmati is Texas-grown Carolina long-grain rice crossed with Thai jasmine rice and our favorite of these aromatic offshoots; it cooks up softer, is snowy white and fragrant, and stays moist longer under refrigeration. It is recommended for rice puddings. All of these rices cook very quickly, like other long-grain white rices, with some rest time

on the Keep Warm steam cycle at the end to set the starch. Look for RiceSelect brand, the marketing arm of RiceTec, Inc., formerly the Farms of Texas Company, the largest private rice research and plant breeding company in the United States. Located in the "rice belt" south of Houston, which covers an area from El Campo to Beaumont on the Gulf of Mexico, RiceTec contracts with small local farmers to grow their proprietary seed (the farms are in various locations to avoid total crop devastation in case of tropical storms). A 14-ounce (390 g) box contains 2 cups (475 ml) of raw rice.

Della rice is our homegrown American aromatic basmati grown in Arkansas, the landlocked area that is not a river delta but the Mississippi River basin, a prairie that is known for how well it holds water, irrigated by extensive ground wells. Decades ago, Lehman Fowler of the Southern Rice Marketing company planted a variety of Indian basmati seed that he adapted for growing conditions in the United States. It is marketed as a white and brown rice under the Della Gourmet trademark of Specialty Rice, Inc. (an offshoot of the now defunct Southern Marketing), along with domestic Arkansas jasmine, Texas Arborio, and domestic Koshi Hikari Japanese rice. Della basmati cooks up nice and dry with distinct grains and is a popular variety to cross with other rices (the different seed stock relatives of Della all have names like Delmont and Delrose, with slightly different characteristics). It is subtle, but still has that nutty basmati taste that is easy to eat alone. Della basmati has been nicknamed "popcorn rice." The most notable American rice offshoots from the Della seed stock are Wild Pecan rice and Louisiana popcorn rice, both with the same faint characteristic perfume.

Short- and Medium-Grain Rices

The kernel of medium-grain rice is oblong and two to three times as long as it is wide. This is the standard rice to use for dessert rice puddings. The kernel of short-grain rice is almost round, but slightly oval, and almost as long as it is wide. It is also referred to as pearl rice. Short-grain white rice is rare to find. When the topic is Asian-style rices, the terms "medium-grain" and "short-grain" are used almost interchangeably. These rices are a must for sushi and rice balls.

AMERICAN RICE

California-grown Calrose, a medium-grain japonica type rice, is the most commonly available medium-grain variety on the West Coast; in the East, southern medium-grain rice from Carolina is on store shelves.

Calrose is typically the lowest priced Japanese-style rice, but its popularity stems from more than its affordability. Like other Japanese-style rices, it has a smooth, moist texture that holds together nicely for chopsticks, and its soothing, mild flavor goes well with spicy foods. This is the rice some people make three times a day fresh for meals, eaten alone, without flavoring. In terms of a bland, clean taste, this rice is probably the best in the world. The kernels cling together and have a comforting tongue appeal. In a pinch, Calrose can be used for sushi (the better brands of Calrose rice can be quite good). One we like, with wide distribution, is Pacific International (formerly Homai).

Calrose was the first Japanese-style rice available in this country, developed by the Rice Development research specialists of the University of California at Davis. It is one of two or three similar varieties grown in California. This rice needs a special temperate climate and is grown only in a few places in the world, including Japan, Korea, Australia, and some countries around the Mediterranean Sea (see Italian Rice). There is no effort to keep the varieties separate during milling and storage in California, so each bag contains a mixture of California rices.

In Asian markets in the United States, where the customers really know rice, price is a good general guide to quality. In fact, at some specialty Asian markets in our own San Francisco Bay Area, the prices of different brands of rice are written on a white board, erased, and rewritten as the market changes. Picky Japanese-American cooks now have many more varieties from which to choose. At the top of the line are Tamaki Gold (our favorite), Tamanishiki, and other "premium" brands; even in large bags, they can cost about $1 a pound. They are great for sushi or special meals. As your rice palate develops, buy a bag of this premium rice to see if you can taste the difference.

Next come popular but more everyday brands with more moderate prices. Kokuhu Rose, Konriko, Nishiki, and other "new variety" rices are delicious examples. The term "new variety" (not the same as "new crop") means it is a high-quality variety of American-grown Japanese-style rice. Many say "new variety" rice is better tasting than Calrose.

If you visit a Japanese market in the United States during the fall and winter months, you are likely to come across a display of banners proclaiming "New Crop Rice Is In." New crop rice is just what it sounds like: the fresh rice from the new harvest. This rice contains more of its natural moisture; use less water to cook it. How much less? Every bag is different, and your first cup (250 ml) of rice from every bag will be your test batch. A general guide is to start off with water about ¼ inch (6 mm) below the correct line on your rice cooker bowl (about 1 to 2 tablespoons [15 to 28 ml] less water per rice cooker cup of rice; 2 to 3 tablespoons [28 to 45 ml] less per U.S. cup of rice). If your rice ends up mushy, reduce the water further; if it's still too chewy at the core, increase the water.

Two coveted and expensive short-grain artisanal rices that were perfected in Japan over two thousand years ago, Koshi Hikari and Akita Komachi, have been planted successfully domestically. Koshi Hikari is being grown in Texas and marketed as sushi rice by RiceSelect and Della Gourmet. If you are a sushi lover or lover of fine Japanese food, you will want to try these short-grain rices. For more information, see Japanese Rice.

Southern medium-grain rice appears to be the same as California medium-grain rice, since its shape and amylose content are the same. But it is not, because it is an *indica* variety, rather than a *japonica*, hence the protein content is a little higher, and it takes longer to cook. If you prefer the Japanese-style medium-grain rices, you will find southern medium-grain rices unacceptable since they cook up drier. Southern medium-grain rice is not as white, not as moist or sticky, and not as clean tasting. This is the type of rice eaten in the southern United States, Louisiana, some parts of Latin America, and Puerto Rico, with black beans, jerked meats, and spicy Caribbean sauces. Good brands include Riceland Plump, Tender Southern Star, Water Maid, and Uncle Ben's Medium Grain (not a converted rice).

ITALIAN RICE

Happily, Italian rice is widely imported today from the Po River region in northern Italy, so an excellent risotto is moments away. Risotto must be made with an Italian-type rice to achieve the proper texture. The rice is intentionally overcooked (by more than 15 minutes). The resulting product has a creamy, starchy surface but a firm bite through the center. Don't rinse or wash Italian rice before cooking; the surface starch contributes to the creamy consistency of risottos, paellas, and puddings.

The most common Italian rice is Arborio, but there are two other lesser known regional varieties, Carnaroli and Vialone nano. Prevean Carnaroli, estate grown and milled in Argentina by the Preve Family of the Po River valley since 1905, is now being imported under the Lotus Foods brand. Arborio has a bigger kernel than regular medium-grain rice, with a distinct chalky center. Carnaroli is the most expensive of the triad and the most difficult to grow. Two domestic brands of Arborio, CalRiso by Lotus Foods and California Arborio by Lundberg, are grown in the Central Valley of California from superfino Arborio seed. Look for the word *superfino* on the package; it is the top grade.

JAPANESE RICE

Japanese rice is not usually exported, but there is no lack of Japanese-style rices, since the American-grown varieties of these rices, like Calrose, are very popular and widely available. In California today there are several Japanese medium- and short-grain varieties being grown that are comparable to two of the most famous and coveted Japanese rices, Akita Komachi and Koshi Hikari, the seeds of which are now being cultivated in small crops in the United States as well.

Just when we had resigned ourselves to the fact that there was no Japanese rice exported, Beth had a sighting at one of our local Japanese markets of the artisanal rice Koshi Hikari, which poetically translates to "rice offering to the gods." The price was steep: $30 for two kilograms (4 lbs, 4 oz). But, of course, we had to have a taste.

Often called the best rice in Japan, Koshi Hikari is the name of the variety, and it is truly an artisanal product, tended and processed with extra care in lots as small as 3 acres (12.1 m²). A short-grain rice, it is grown in Nigata prefecture, a small coastal area in central Japan on the Sea of Japan that is renowned for the quality of its rice. We found beautiful rice-paper bags of Koshi Hikari rice for sale around January and New Year's, a prime season for gift-giving. It was delicious, a beautiful pearlescent oval, and very similar in flavor, texture, and style to our favorite U.S.–grown Japanese-style brand, Tamaki Gold. It is prepared in exactly the same way as other Japanese-style short- and medium-grain rices and is excellent for eating rice bowl style and for sushi.

Tamaki Gold, packaged by the Williams Rice Milling Company, is 100 percent Koshi Hikari. Less expensive Tamaki Classic is a blend of two varieties: the premium Akita Komachi and California Hikari.

If you want to try some of the world's best imported Koshi Hikari sushi rice, you can mail-order it from Williams-Sonoma under the label of Kumai Harvest.

SPANISH RICE

Spanish-grown rice is labeled paella or Valencia rice (*arroz alla Valenciana*). Cultivated on the Mediterranean coast of Spain in Valencia and the Ebro River delta, it is increasingly available in this country. Other medium-grain rices can be substituted beautifully for this rice.

The other well-known Spanish rice is the unique Calasparra. A large-grained japonica called *bomba*, because of its size, it is now readily available from Williams-Sonoma. It is expensive because it is grown in only one small region outside of Valencia, stamped with a *denominación del origen*, a region of origin, like the rices imported from Japan. It is considered an artisanal rice by gourmet standards and is used to make paella. Be prepared for it to soak up a lot of liquid, more than you have ever seen a rice absorb, needed to soften the grains.

INDIAN RICE

When shopping in an Indian foods market, we found an astonishing array of miniature grain rices imported from various areas of India. While unfamiliar to most American cooks, these rices have their own charm and uses in regional cooking. Kalijira is a miniature basmati-type medium-grain white rice imported exclusively by Lotus Foods, and is the diminutive rice that has crossed over into specialty supermarkets. Like all true basmatis, its little needle-like grain elongates as it cooks, but plumps like a medium-grain rice at the same time. It is an ancient strain grown in Bangladesh and is so expensive that it is reserved only for holiday meals in that country. It is also grown across the border in Bengal, India, where it is known as *gobindavog*. Use Kalijira for special pilafs and dessert puddings.

EGYPTIAN RICE

Egyptian-grown rice is a medium-grain japonica cultivated in the marshy Nile waters and is used for Turkish-style pilafs. While the grains are smaller than those of Arborio, they look similar, but cook up more like Japanese-style medium-grain rice. It is sold in Middle Eastern specialty food stores.

SWEET RICE

Sweet rice, also known as sticky, waxy, glutinous, pearl, or California mochi rice (it is known as *mochi gome* in Japan), is a real specialty item. These names are deceptive since sweet rice is only slightly sweeter than conventional rice, so most palates would not detect any sweetness. The nature of the starch is that it contains almost pure amylopectin, so the rice is very sticky indeed. Sweet rice is a *japonica* rice, and a few acres in California are dedicated to this variety. It is usually steamed and used to make Asian-style desserts, stuffings, and cakes. It can also be made into noodles and sake, or ground into flour. A good brand is Honen sweet rice, which can be found in Asian markets and larger supermarkets.

Brown Rices

Brown rice is the earthy sibling of white rice. It is the same grain as white rice, but is simply left unhulled, so it looks tan. Brown rice always takes at least twice the amount of time to cook as white rice and a bit more water since the grains need to absorb more to soften. The thick bran layer is coated with a waxy layer that is very difficult for moisture to penetrate; requirements for cooking and soaking times are dramatically increased, though the boiling/steaming process remains the same. Because of these bran layers, brown rice has more fiber, which makes it chewy, with a great, distinctive flavor. Because of its retention of natural vitamins and minerals, this is the rice called for in special high-fiber and vegetarian diets. Since any pesticides and fungicides that are used during the growing remain as residue in the bran layer, many cooks seek out organic brands.

Natural brown rice comes in long-, medium-, and short-grain varieties, as well as a number of specialty and heirloom varieties. We found that most aromatic varieties, like Wild Pecan rice and imported brown basmati, taste quite similar, while the California-grown brown rices are less complex but nuttier, although every bit as satisfying.

Short-grain brown rices include Lundberg's California-grown Natural Short-Grain Brown Rice, Kokuho Rose Brown Rice, Calrose, and Hinode Brown Rice. Long-grain brown rices include imported brown basmati, domestic brown jasmine (from Lowell Farms), Lundberg Long-Grain Brown Rice, and brown Della and Texmati rices. Pacific International (formerly Homai) markets both California-grown grades. While the Japanese traditionally eat only white rice (given rations of brown rice, "poor people's rice," after World War II, locals polished the rice with their home milling equipment rather than eat brown rice), this is changing. At our last shopping visit to the Japanese market, there were stacks of 10- and 20-pound (4.6 and 9.1 kg) plastic bags of both long- and medium-grain organic California-grown brown rices, simply labeled as such.

Short- and medium-grain brown rices are good for casseroles, salads, dinner rice, stuffings, unorthodox sushi, and stir-fries. Long-grain brown rices are good in casseroles, fried rice, salads, soups, waffles and pancakes, side dishes, and pilafs.

RED RICE

There are dozens of red rices grown around the world, but they are relatively new to the American gourmet rice eater. Though technically a brown rice, instead of a brown hull, red rices have a pink to red to mahogany hull. Red rices cook in a manner similar to that of other brown or medium-grain rices, and have a distinctly nutty, almost popcorn-like aroma and a distinctly nutty flavor.

Wehani (an Indian red rice hybrid developed by Lundberg) is a plump long-grain red rice that has been improved to cook up less sticky than regular brown rices. Wehani and a rice called Richvale Red are mixed to make Lundberg's Christmas Blend. Lotus Foods imports a red rice from Bhutan, and in some specialty markets you can find Thai red rice, South Indian red rice (*rosematta*), Vietnamese (cargo) red rice, and Himalayan red rice.

French red rice has a gourmet following and is often served in three-star restaurants. Planted in 1942 by the Chinese and Madagascarean military troops fighting in France, the marshy lands on the Mediterranean have been desalinated and developed into an artisan rice colony, with both medium-grain red and organic brown rices grown; at this writing, these rices are rarely imported. If you are traveling in Provence, France, you may encounter a red rice grown in the Rhône delta of the Camargue, *riz rouge de Camargue*.

BLACK RICE

Black and purple-black rices are considered brown rices because they are unhulled (underneath the hull they are white when polished), leaving the colored hull layers intact. While this color rice is highly unusual in America, there are hundreds of varieties of black rice in Asia. They are common in southern China, the highlands of Southeast Asia, Bali, and parts of Indonesia. Black rice is a *japonica*, so it cooks up sticky and is eaten with the fingers. It is also a familiar temple and festival offering for special religious holidays. Domestic Black Japonica (from Lundberg) was the first recognizable black rice in America; it has an assertive flavor, like that of wild rice. For that reason, Lundberg mixes it into blends such as Wild Blend and Gourmet Blend of 7 Brown Rices; they are not only delicious, but work beautifully in the rice cooker. Thai black rice, which is not really sticky, is not often seen in the United States; it is mixed with white rice and dyes the whole pot purple-black. Thai black rice is especially good for desserts. The newest black rice to be marketed in the U.S. is Forbidden Rice (China black), grown in Zhezhiang in northern China and imported by Lotus Foods. It has become popular as an alternative to regular white rice in California-style cuisine and restaurants. It is not a sticky rice, which makes this rice unique. It is a rice bowl rice and used to make congee, the beloved Chinese savory breakfast porridge.

A Recipe Formula for Every Rice

The rice cooker is, in most cases, used exclusively for making plain white rices cooked in water. While experienced cooks can dump some rice into a pot and estimate the amount of water by eye or "knuckle deep" feel (½ inch [1.3 cm] above the rice by "eye"), some of us need a bit more help, such as a proportion chart and measuring cup. Every home cook, and professional cook, agrees that getting the proportions right is often a challenge (sometimes even the proportions on the bag are not quite right). We have provided them here, for every type of rice, for your convenience.

Each of the three charts on the following pages has amounts suitable for all three sizes of machines: 3- to 4-cup (700 to 946 ml) (known as "small"), 5- to 6-cup (1.2 to 1.4 L) (known as "medium"), and 8- to 10-cup (1.9 to 2.4 L) (known as "large"). While there are rice cookers that are downright gigantic and used in restaurants, we have focused on the sizes available to the home cook. There is a chart for each category of rice: brown rice (page 33), long (page 34), and medium (page 34).

We recommend that when you first make rice in your rice cooker, you use the amounts and guidelines stated in the manual accompanying your machine. If you are not happy with the results, then refer to our charts. We were astonished to find that every rice cooker cooked rice just a little bit differently, and each cook likes his or her rice just so, so plan on a bit of experimentation to get your rice just as you like it.

How much to make and in what size machine? If you live alone, a small rice cooker is perfect. For 2 to 6 people, use a 5- to 6-cup (1.2 to 1.4 L) model (it cooks even 1 rice cooker cup of raw rice perfectly), and if you have a larger family or make rice for company and large salads, get a large 10-cup (2.4 L) cooker. The 10-cup (2.4 L) model does not make 1 cup (235 ml) of raw rice efficiently; you must make 2 cups (475 ml) minimum or it will cook up too dry. Some rice cooker aficionados own two sizes.

A basic guide when deciding how much rice to make is to remember that rice doubles or triples in volume after cooking, so 1 cup (235 ml) of raw rice cooks up into 2 to 3 cups (475 to 700 ml) of cooked rice. How much you need will be determined by how you will be eating. Will it be a side dish, part of the main dish with a topping, or the main dish itself? Is it for a salad and do you want leftovers?

HOW TO USE THE RICE CHARTS

The most common use of the rice cooker is to cook plain rice, and most people, most of the time, will be cooking long-grain white rice, medium-grain white rice, or brown rice. Each of these types takes different amounts of water, and the amounts can vary based on the size of the rice cooker, since rice cooks differently in every type of cooking vessel (depth and width of the pot, weight of the material the pot is made out of, and how tight the cover is are all factors). That's why we put together these charts—to help you make perfect rice, whatever your favorite variety and whatever the size of your rice cooker.

In every case, we recommend starting out with the amounts of water and rice suggested by the manufacturer of your rice cooker. If you are dissatisfied, try the measurements here. In our testing, we found that those handy calibrations on the rice cooker bowls are not always correct, or at least they didn't always correspond to the way we liked the rice cooked. If the rice is still not to your liking, continue to tinker, adding or reducing the water about ¼ cup (60 ml) at a time until your cooker is turning out rice that is perfectly suited to your tastes, jotting down the results. If your rice is too chewy, increase the amount of water; if it's too mushy or soggy, decrease the water. Some do like it chewier, some like it softer. And in the end, your preferences are the ones that matter.

Also, please be aware that increasing and decreasing rice proportions is downright tricky. Short- and medium-grain rices always need less water than long-grain. And as the amount of rice increases, the proportion of necessary water or cooking liquid decreases. You will be able to use our charts to help determine correct proportions for the recipes in this book.

Looking at the chart, first determine how many servings of rice you want to make. The amounts of rice in the charts are listed first in rice cooker cups, with the equivalent measurement in U.S. cups shown in the next column, so you can measure either way. Then read across the chart to find the amount of water to add under the size of your machine. The water is measured in U.S. cups (8 fluid ounces = 1 cup [235 ml]). Please measure the water carefully, at eye level, in a liquid measuring cup (the kind with a handle and pouring spout and calibrations on the side, usually made of Pyrex rather than metal).

Notice that the amount of water differs based on the size of the rice cooker, because of the amount of surface evaporation, with the larger cooker obviously having the most surface area. Cooking small amounts of rice in the large machine is not advised; it will end up too dry and tough. Add the water to the rice in the rice cooker. Then close the rice cooker and turn it on. When the machine finishes cooking, be sure to let the rice steam for 10 to 15 minutes on the Keep Warm cycle (or in the closed rice cooker, if you have the on/off type) before opening the cooker, stirring the rice with the rice paddle, and serving. (In fuzzy logic rice cookers, the steaming period is built in, but a short rest on Keep Warm is still recommended.)

BROWN RICE (MEDIUM-GRAIN OR LONG-GRAIN)

Serves	Rice		Water (in U.S. Cups)		
	Rice Cooker Cups	(Equivalent in U.S. Cups)	Small (4-Cup) Rice Cooker	Medium (6-cup [1.4 L]) Rice Cooker	Large (10-Cup) Rice Cooker
2	1	¾ (175 ml)	1¾ (410 ml)	1¾ (410 ml)	2¼ (535 ml)
4	2	1½ (335 ml)	2½ (570 ml)	2½ (570 ml)	3⅓ (780 ml)
6	3	2¼ (535 ml)	3⅔ (860 ml)	3⅔ (860 ml)	4½ (1.1 L)
8	4	3 (700 ml)		4⅔ (1.1 L)	5⅓ (1.3 L)
10	5	3¾ (875 ml)			6½ (1.5 L)
12	6	4½ (1.1 L)			7½ (1.8 L)

AMERICAN LONG-GRAIN WHITE RICE

Serves	Rice	Water (in U.S. Cups)			
	Rice Cooker Cups	(Equivalent in U.S. Cups)	Small (4-Cup) Rice Cooker	Medium (6-cup [1.4 L]) Rice Cooker	Large (10-Cup) Rice Cooker
2	1	¾ (175 ml)	1¼ (285 ml)	1¼ (285 ml)	1¼ (285 ml)
4	2	1½ (355 ml)	2⅛ (500 ml)	2⅛ (500 ml)	2¼ (538 ml)
6	3	2¼ (535 ml)	3 (700 ml)	3⅛ (735 ml)	3¼ (760 ml)
8	4	3 (700 ml)	3⅔ (860 ml)	3¾ (875 ml)	4 (946 ml)
10	5	3¾ (825 ml)		4½ (1.1 L)	4¾ (1.1 L)
12	6	4½ (1.1 L)		5½ (1.3 L)	5½ (1.3 L)
14	7	5¼ (1.2 L)			6½ (1.5 L)
16	8	6 (1.4 L)			7½ (1.8 L)
18	9	6¾ (1.6 L)			8½ (2 L)
20	10	7½ (1.8 L)			9½ (2.2 L)

MEDIUM-GRAIN WHITE RICE

Serves	Rice	Water (in U.S. Cups)			
	Rice Cooker Cups	(Equivalent in U.S. Cups)	Small (4-Cup) Rice Cooker	Medium (6-cup [1.4 L]) Rice Cooker	Large (10-Cup) Rice Cooker
2	1	¾ (175 ml)	1¼ (285 ml)	1¼ (285 ml)	1½ (355 ml)
4	2	1½ (355 ml)	2 (475 ml)	2 (475 ml)	2⅛ (500 ml)
6	3	2¼ (535 ml)	2¾ (700 ml)	3 (700 ml)	3 (700 ml)
8	4	3 (700 ml)	3½ (820 ml)	3⅔ (860 ml)	3⅔ (860 ml)
10	5	3¾ (875 ml)		4¼ (1 L)	4⅓ (1 L)
12	6	4½ (1.1 L)		5¼ (1.2 L)	5¼ (1.2 L)
14	7	5¼ (1.2 L)			6 (1.4 L)
16	8	6 (1.4 L)			7 (1.6 L)
18	9	6¾ (1.6 L)			8 (1.9 L)
20	10	7½ (1.8 L)			9 (2.1 L)

American Long-Grain White Rice

▶ MACHINE: Medium (6-cup [1.4 L]) rice cooker; fuzzy logic or on/off ▶ CYCLE: Regular ▶ YIELD: Serves 3 to 4

The Japanese-made rice cooker was developed specifically to cook the rices most often cooked in their cuisine: medium- and short-grain white rices. So long-grain white rice is sometimes a bit of a challenge to get just right in the rice cooker. Long-grain rice is preferred in Chinese diets, as well as most of the other rice-oriented cuisines, such as in the Philippines, India, and South America. American cooks also prefer long-grain rices.

This recipe is for regular domestic long-grain white rice, brands like Mahatma and Pacific International, and the non-aromatic Indian extra-long-grain white rice (look for the finest grade, called *Patna*, for the region in which it is grown). The package will indicate whether it is grown in Texas, Arkansas, or California, our main regions for growing the offshoots of our original Carolina gold strain of rice. Domestic long-grain white rice does not have to be washed or soaked before cooking, but the extra-long-grain Indian rice should have one rinse. (Note: This recipe is *not* for imported aromatic rices like basmati or jasmine.)

1 cup (185 g) long-grain white rice
1½ cups (355 ml) water
¼ teaspoon salt
1 to 2 tablespoons (14 to 28 g) unsalted butter, margarine, olive oil, or nut oil (optional)

1. Place the rice in the rice cooker bowl. Add the water and salt; swirl to combine. Close the cover and set for the Regular cycle.

2. When the machine switches to the Keep Warm cycle, let the rice steam for 10 minutes. Fluff the rice with a wooden or plastic rice paddle or wooden spoon. This rice will hold on Keep Warm for hours.

3. Before serving, stir in the butter or oil, if using. Serve hot.

Chinese-Style Plain Rice

▶ MACHINE: Medium (6-cup [1.4 L]) rice cooker; fuzzy logic or on/off ▶ CYCLE: Regular ▶ YIELD: Serves 3 to 4

**1 cup (185 g) long-grain
white rice
1¼ cups (285 ml) water**

Ancient Chinese cooks were given the same social rank as esteemed painters and poets, and one especially important dish they had to make was *fan,* or Chinese white rice, to be served alongside multiple savory dishes. Besides long-grain white rice, Chinese recipes can call for long-grain brown rice (as an alternative to white rice in stir-fries and as an everyday rice), glutinous sticky rice (for stuffings and dumplings), or short-grain white rice, for everyday eating and the savory breakfast porridge, congee. It is always made without salt to properly complement the soy sauce and other complex flavoring condiments in the food. Please note that the rice is not finished cooking until after sitting for 15 minutes on the Keep Warm cycle.

1. Place the rice in a bowl, rinse with cold water, and pour the water off, taking care to keep the rice in the bottom of the bowl. Rinse one to three more times, if desired.

2. Coat the rice cooker bowl with nonstick cooking spray or a film of vegetable oil. Place the rice in the rice bowl. Add the water, close the cover, and set for the Regular cycle.

3. When the machine switches to the Keep Warm cycle, let the rice steam for 15 minutes. Fluff the rice with a wooden or plastic rice paddle or wooden spoon. This rice will hold on Keep Warm for hours. Serve hot.

4. *Chinese jasmine rice:* Place the water in the rice cooker bowl. Add 1 teaspoon loose jasmine tea leaves and a dash of salt to the water; let stand for 3 minutes to steep. Add the rinsed and drained rice, swirl to evenly distribute, and cook the rice as directed. You could also use a jasmine tea bag and remove it before you begin cooking the rice, but the bits of tea leaves in the cooked rice are very nice. Great with soy-and-ginger-marinated chicken or fish.

5. *Chinese restaurant rice:* Coat the rice bowl with 1 teaspoon Asian sesame oil. Substitute ¼ cup (50 g) short-grain rice for ¼ cup (46 g) of the long-grain rice (the ratio is 3 parts long-grain white rice to 1 part short-grain rice).

Converted Rice

Parboiling rice is a technique that was invented in ancient India (and still preferred in the humid areas of southern India and Bangladesh). Rice is boiled still in its husk, which keeps it from swelling, kills the microscopic larva in the germ of every grain, and pushes the nutrients in the outer layers into the center of the grain. The grain hardens slightly (making it easy to polish by hand) and is sterilized. The process even mends cracks in the rice (the starch glues broken rice back together), making for a higher yield. The rice is then dried unhusked (known as paddy rice), and passed through a standard milling process to remove the hull and bran. Once milled, the rice can be safely stored for long periods without losing any of its inherent nutrition and is resistant to bugs.

In this country, parboiled rice is known as converted rice. Converted rice, under the trademark of Uncle Ben's, is long-grain white rice that has been parboiled by steaming it under pressure, and then is refined by removing the hull, bran, and germ. It was developed for use in the overseas armed forces kitchens during World War II. It is the only type of rice that can withstand the harsh treatment of most industrial processes that involve cooking and then freezing, canning, or drying and, for that reason, it is the rice used in most boxed mixes. It has more nutrition than plain white rice, since it is enriched, and takes longer to cook than regular white rice because the starch is slightly hardened and needs more liquid to soften.

While most cooks say, "No, thank you," to converted rice because so many other long-grain white rices are available, we love it for certain dishes. It cooks up perfectly, with the most distinct grains and the least amount of stickiness of any of the rices. Because of this, converted rice is excellent for use in rice salads, absorbing dressings and not becoming mushy. It is the rice of choice for dishes such as jambalaya. It is good in pilafs and, to our great surprise, is the most used rice in Paris after imported Thai jasmine.

Here is a guide to making converted rice in your rice cooker, from 2 to 22 servings, since the rice/liquid proportions vary so drastically and this is the perfect rice to make in quantity.

▶ MACHINE: Small (4-cup) rice cooker; fuzzy logic or on/off ▶ CYCLE: Regular ▶ YIELD: Serves 2

½ cup (94 g) converted rice
1 cup (235 ml) plus 2 tablespoons (28 ml) water

2 teaspoons unsalted butter (optional)
Pinch of salt

(Continued on next page)

▶ MACHINE: Small (4-cup) or medium (6-cup [1.4 L]) rice cooker; fuzzy logic or on/off ▶ YIELD: Serves 4

1 cup (188 g) converted rice	1 tablespoon (14 g) unsalted butter (optional)
2 cups (475 ml) water	¼ teaspoon salt

▶ MACHINE: Medium (6-cup [1.4 L]) rice cooker; fuzzy logic or on/off ▶ YIELD: Serves 6

1½ cups (282 g) converted rice	1½ tablespoons (21 g) unsalted butter
3 cups (700 ml) water	(optional)

¾ teaspoon salt

▶ MACHINE: Medium (6-cup [1.4 L]) or large (10-cup) rice cooker; fuzzy logic or on/off ▶ YIELD: Serves 12

Note: This is the largest volume of cooked rice that will fit in the medium rice cooker.

3 cups (564 g) converted rice	2½ tablespoons (35 g) unsalted butter (optional)
5 cups (1.2 L) water	1½ teaspoons salt

▶ MACHINE: Large (10-cup) rice cooker; fuzzy logic or on/off ▶ YIELD: Serves 22

6 cups (1.1 kg) converted rice	5 tablespoons (70 g) unsalted butter (optional)
9½ cups (2.2 L) water	1 tablespoon (18 g) salt

1. Place the rice in the rice cooker bowl. Add the water, butter, if using, and salt; swirl to combine. Close the cover and set for the Regular cycle.

2. When the machine switches to the Keep Warm cycle, let the rice steam for 10 minutes.

3. Fluff the rice with a wooden or plastic rice paddle or wooden spoon. This rice keeps perfectly on Keep Warm for at least 2 hours.

Basmati Rice

▶ MACHINE: Medium (6-cup [1.4 L]) rice cooker; fuzzy logic or on/off ▶ CYCLE: Regular ▶ YIELD: Serves 4

Basmati is ever so delightfully delicate both in texture and flavor. It gives credence to the label "aromatic" rice. The best grades are Dehraduni and Patna basmati, but just look in the box: the rather small, needle-like grains should all be whole, rather than broken. Basmati is aged from six months to a year in burlap sacks layered with neem leaves—an ancient tree native to East India that is a natural insecticide—to dry it out and develop its flavor; basmati should never smell musty. As it cooks, the grain elongates up to three times its length, rather than plumping out. Basmati cooks in a very short time, around 30 minutes usually, depending on the freshness of the rice (older rice will take longer). This is also the recipe to use for domestic Della white basmati, Lundberg white basmati, and the lesser known imported Indian Tohfa and Kohinoor basmatis.

1 cup (180 g) basmati rice
1½ cups (355 ml) water
¼ teaspoon fine sea salt

1. Place the rice in a bowl and fill with cold water. Swish it around with your fingers. Bits of grain will float to the top; the water will foam around the edges and become murky. Carefully pour off the water and rinse a second time. If the rice water is still murky, rinse and drain again; basmati usually takes two to four rinsings. Discard the rinse water. An optional step is to let the basmati air-dry in the strainer for 30 minutes or to soak it in a bowl, covered with cold water, for 30 minutes. Drain well. (Traditional recipes call for the basmati to be cooked in its soaking liquid. If you'd like, you can pour this off into a measuring cup and use it for cooking.)

2. Place the rice in the rice cooker bowl. Add the water and salt; swirl to combine. Close the cover and set for the Regular cycle.

3. When the machine switches to the Keep Warm cycle, let the rice steam for 10 minutes. Fluff the rice with a wooden or plastic rice paddle or wooden spoon. This rice will hold on Keep Warm for hours. Serve hot.

American Jasmine Rice

▶ MACHINE: Medium (6-cup [1.4 L]) rice cooker; fuzzy logic or on/off ▶ CYCLE: Regular ▶ YIELD: Serves 6 to 8

2 cups (360 g) domestic
    white jasmine rice
3 cups (700 ml) water
Large pinch of fine sea salt
    (optional)

American jasmine rice is exclusively grown for and distributed by Lotus Foods under the Lowell Farms label. We got this recipe from the company founder, Caryl Levine, who not only searches out exceptional imported and domestic rices, but eats rice every day out of her 10-cup rice cooker. The organic jasmine rice grown in El Campo, Texas, is a variety developed by the International Rice Institute in the Philippines and Texas A & M University. American jasmine is less processed than imported Thai jasmine, so it will take a bit more time to cook and, as you will note from the proportions, a bit more water. Caryl always likes a bit of salt. "It brings out the best in rice," she says. A great everyday rice you just might end up liking better than the imported variety.

1. Place the rice in a fine strainer or bowl, rinse with cold water, and drain.

2. Coat the rice cooker bowl with nonstick cooking spray or a film of vegetable oil. Place the rice in the rice bowl. Add the water and salt, if using; swirl to combine. Close the cover and set for the Regular cycle.

3. When the machine switches to the Keep Warm cycle, let the rice steam for 15 minutes. Fluff the rice with a wooden or plastic rice paddle or wooden spoon. This rice will hold on Keep Warm for hours. Serve hot.

Thai Jasmine Rice

▸ MACHINE: Medium (6-cup [1.4 L]) rice cooker; fuzzy logic or on/off ▸ CYCLE: Regular ▸ YIELD: Serves 6 to 8

2 cups (360 g) Thai
 jasmine rice
2¼ cups (535 ml) water
¼ teaspoon salt

The word for rice in Thai is *kao,* and the type of rice found all over the country is a pearl-white long-grain rice labeled Thai jasmine. It has a plump, elongated shape, not round like short-grain rice or thin and long like American long-grain. The rice cooks up fluffy and moist, with a delicate floral aroma that is a favorite with many cooks in many nations. Many brands are labeled Riz Parfumé. Considered the most delicate grain of all the rices, it is harvested in December during the dry months and is marketed fresh. Thai jasmine loses its fragrance as the raw rice ages, so often it is stored in the refrigerator.

Many cooks complain that their jasmine rice is too gummy after cooking; that is because they are cooking it in too much water. Thai jasmine is not the same as long-grain Thai sticky rice, *kao neuw,* which is prepared in the north of the country, steamed in a spittoon-shaped rice pot, and eaten only with the hands.

1. Place the rice in a fine strainer or bowl, rinse with cold water until the water runs clear, and drain.

2. Coat the rice cooker bowl with nonstick cooking spray or a film of vegetable oil. Place the rice in the rice bowl. Add the water and salt; swirl to combine. Close the cover and set for the Regular cycle.

3. When the machine switches to the Keep Warm cycle, let the rice steam for 15 minutes. Fluff the rice with a wooden or plastic rice paddle or wooden spoon. This rice holds nicely on Keep Warm for up to 3 hours. Serve hot.

4. Note: If the cooked rice seems too dry, add a bit more water (up to 2 to 3 tablespoons [28 to 45 ml]) and leave it on the Keep Warm cycle for 15 minutes to continue steaming.

Medium-Grain White Rice

▶ MACHINE: Medium (6-cup [1.4 L]) rice cooker; fuzzy logic or on/off ▶ CYCLE: Regular ▶ YIELD: Serves 3 to 4

1 cup (195 g) medium-grain white rice
1⅓ cups (315 ml) water
¼ teaspoon salt (optional)

This is the recipe to use for basic steamed rice or the Japanese daily rice, *okame*, made from the white rice known as *seihakumai*. Remember, if you bought a bag of rice labeled "new crop," *shinmai* (which is fresh every autumn), you will decrease the ratio of water to rice to 1:1 (that will be 1 cup [235 ml] of water here). The method of washing described below is more extensive than what many cooks actually do. If you're pressed for time, just swish and drain a few times. If your rice is labeled "Musenmai" or "Rinse-free rice," the washing is optional. (If you don't wash it, use a bit more water.) This recipe is geared to domestic medium-grain white rice, which is grown in either California or Arkansas. Use brands like Nishiki, Homai, Botan, Konriko, Tamaki Classic, and southern medium-grain brands, *not* domestic or imported Arborios. These are the same proportions to use for *haiga mai*, partially polished white rice. For 1½ cups (293 g) rice, use 2 cups (475 ml) water.

1. Wash the rice. Place the rice in a bowl and fill the bowl about half-full with cold water. Swirl the rice in the water with your hand. Carefully pour off most of the water, through a mesh strainer or by holding one cupped hand under the stream to catch any grains of rice that are carried away with the water. Holding the bowl steady with one hand, use the other to rub and squeeze the wet rice, turning the bowl as you go so that all the rice is "scrubbed." The small amount of water in the bowl will turn chalky white. Now, run cold water into the bowl, give the rice a quick swish, and carefully drain off the water as before. Repeat the scrubbing and pouring-off process twice more. By the third time, the water you pour off will be nearly clear.

2. Place the rice in the rice cooker bowl. Add the water and salt, if using; swirl to combine. Let the rice soak for 30 minutes to 1 hour with the cover shut, time permitting. At the end of the soaking period, set for the Regular cycle.

3. When the machine switches to the Keep Warm cycle, let the rice steam for 15 minutes. Gently but thoroughly fluff the rice with a plastic or wooden rice paddle or wooden spoon. This rice will hold on Keep Warm for hours. Serve hot.

Reheating Rice in the Rice Cooker

Some cooks make extra rice and have it for a day or two in the refrigerator, ready for quick meals. Other cooks would never think of using day-old rice. In case you need to reheat some rice, here's how.

Place the cold rice in the rice cooker bowl. Add 1 to 2 tablespoons water (old rice will need a bit more water, new rice less) and break up the stiff clumps of cold rice. Cover and program for Regular cycle. Steam until the timer sounds, about 10 minutes. Eat immediately and do not reheat again.

Japanese White Rice with Umeboshi and Sesame

▶ YIELD: Serves 2 to 3

Tart and salty, pinky-red umeboshi pickled plums are an acquired taste to some. To others, it is just another comfort food along with miso. Anyone who has taken a macrobiotic cooking class gets hooked on umeboshi. On a visit to Japantown, our lunch boxes always have a bright, shriveled pickled plum plunked into the mound of fresh white rice. Prepare the condiments while the rice is cooking; you want to be ready to serve as soon as the rice has finished on the Keep Warm cycle. Umeboshi plums are sold in Asian groceries and natural foods stores. This recipe—inspired by Hiroko Shimbo, author of *The Japanese Kitchen* (Harvard Common Press, 2000)—has quickly become a favorite quick lunch on the run.

2 umeboshi plums, pitted and minced

2 tablespoons (8 g) minced fresh Italian parsley leaves

1½ tablespoons (8 g) toasted Japanese sesame seeds (see note below)

3 cups (558 g) hot cooked medium-grain white rice

Sesame oil (not toasted), for drizzling

Tamari (a thick, strong soy sauce; reduced-sodium, if desired), for drizzling

1. Place the umeboshi, parsley, and sesame seeds in separate small, shallow serving bowls.

2. Place the rice in a medium-size serving bowl, sprinkle it with the condiments, and drizzle with some sesame oil and tamari. Serve immediately.

Note: Japanese sesame seeds are sold toasted; you can toast them again in a dry skillet for more flavor.

Riso

▶ MACHINE: Medium (6-cup [1.4 L]) rice cooker; fuzzy logic or on/off ▶ CYCLE: Regular
▶ YIELD: Serves 4 (about 3½ cups [650 g])

1¼ cups (225 g) Arborio,
  Carnaroli, or Vialone nano
  rice
1¾ cups (410 ml) water
1 tablespoon (15 ml) olive
  oil
Small pinch of salt

Riso is Italian for rice, and Italian rice is domestic or imported Arborio, Carnaroli, or Vialone nano. While these rices are commonly cooked into a risotto, the side dish that is like a creamy savory rice pudding, "everyday" rice is cooked so that the grains are dry and separate, more like a pilaf than a risotto. Home recipes for *riso* require the cook to measure the same amount of dry rice and water plus ½ cup (120 ml) extra water for the cooking pot. We found the measurements ran true when translating the recipe to the rice cooker. This rice takes a long time to cook for white rice, a full hour. Be prepared for the rice to be ever-so-slightly chewy in a percentage of the grains. One look and you will recognize the perfect example of a plumped medium-sized grain of rice. It is slightly moist, but dry on the tongue, and very tasty without being sweet. Serve with butter and Parmesan cheese as a side like any other rice bowl rice, or as a bed for sautéed meat and onions. This is the rice to make for stuffed peppers, stuffings, rice omelets, fritters, and Italian rice and vegetable salads dressed with olive oil and lemon juice.

1. Place the rice in the rice cooker bowl. Add the water, olive oil, and salt; swirl to combine. Close the cover and set for the Regular cycle.

2. When the machine switches to the Keep Warm cycle, let the rice steam for 10 minutes. Fluff the rice gently with a wooden or plastic rice paddle or wooden spoon. This rice will hold on Keep Warm for hours. Serve hot.

Short-Grain White Rice

Short-grain rice makes the best sushi. It is also called pearl rice, especially in dessert recipes. Traditional cooking methods require soaking to get a nice soft texture. There is a lot of starch in short-grain rice, so it really sticks together after cooking, but deliciously so. It is a type of rice that tastes better with every bite. Our favorite brand of Japanese-style rice, Tamaki Gold, is labeled short-grain. "What were the proportions to get that Tamaki Gold so perfect?" Beth asked Julie one day. "Three rice cooker cups and water to the line that says 3 on the bowl, just the way the machine was designed to cook." This recipe gives measurements in U.S. cups, but if you use the white rice recipe from the manufacturer's pamphlet, measurements will be in rice cooker cups. This is the recipe to use for imported and domestic Koshi Hikari.

1. Place the rice in a bowl and fill about half-full with cold water. Swirl the rice in the water with your hand. Carefully pour off most of the water, through a mesh strainer or by holding one cupped hand under the stream to catch any grains of rice that are carried away with the water. Holding the bowl steady with one hand, use the other to rub and squeeze the wet rice, turning the bowl as you go so that all the rice is "scrubbed." The small amount of water in the bowl will turn chalky white. Now, run cold water into the bowl, give the rice a quick swish, and carefully drain off the water as before. Repeat the scrubbing and pouring-off process twice more. By the third time, the water you pour off will be nearly clear.

2. Place the rice in the rice cooker bowl. Add the water (to line 2) and salt, if using; swirl to combine. Let the rice soak for 30 minutes to 1 hour in the bowl with the cover shut, time permitting. When the soaking period is finished, set for the Regular cycle.

3. When the machine switches to the Keep Warm cycle, gently but thoroughly fluff the rice with a wooden or plastic rice paddle or wooden spoon. Let the rice steam for 10 to 15 minutes. This rice will hold on Keep Warm for hours. Serve hot.

1½ cups (300 g) 2 rice cooker cups short-grain white rice

1⅔ cups (395 ml) cold water

¼ teaspoon salt (optional)

Steamed Sticky Rice

▶ MACHINE: Medium (6-cup [1.4 L]) or large (10-cup) rice cooker; on/off only ▶ CYCLE: Regular
▶ YIELD: Serves 4 to 6

2¼ cups (3 rice cooker cups) sticky rice
1 teaspoon salt

These instructions for steamed sticky rice come courtesy of Hiroko Shimbo, author of the encyclopedic and accessible book *The Japanese Kitchen* (Harvard Common Press, 2000). Not everyone salts their sticky rice before cooking; feel free to leave out the salt if you wish. Hiroko notes that sticky rice is often served for special occasions, topped with a sprinkle of *gomasio*, the addictive sesame seed and salt condiment. She explains that you can make your own by toasting 3 tablespoons (24 g) black sesame seeds in a small skillet over low heat until fragrant. If you wish, you can release more of the seeds' fragrance and flavor by partly grinding them with a mortar and pestle or the Japanese ridged *suribachi*, made for precisely that purpose. Add 2 teaspoons sea salt to the sesame seeds and let the mixture cool.

You need an on/off rice cooker with a steamer basket or tray that fits into the top of the cooker. When steaming sticky rice, the steamer basket or tray must be lined with a piece of cloth, which is then folded over to enclose the rice. You can use a double or triple layer of cheesecloth, a square of muslin, or a cloth made especially for this purpose, which is sold in Japanese markets. We have also used a clean linen handkerchief with great success. If you love rice, treat yourself to making this rice and enjoy the texture achieved by the steaming.

1. Wash the rice. Place the rice in a bowl (or use the bowl of your rice cooker) and fill the bowl about half-full with cold tap water. Swirl the rice in the water with your hand. Carefully pour off most of the water, holding one cupped hand under the stream to catch any grains of rice that are carried away with the water. Holding the bowl steady with one hand, use the other to rub and squeeze the wet rice, turning the bowl as you go, so that all the rice is "scrubbed."

2. The small amount of water in the bowl will turn chalky white. Now, run cold water into the bowl, give the rice a quick swish, and carefully drain off the water as before. Repeat the scrubbing and pouring-off process two more times. By the third time, the water you pour off will be nearly clear.

3. Place the drained rice in a bowl and add cold water to cover by several inches (13 to 18 cm). Let the rice soak at room temperature for at least 3 hours, and overnight if possible.

4. Drain the rice, discarding the water. Add the salt to the rice and toss it gently to mix. Fill the rice cooker bowl about half-full of water. Close the cover and set for the Regular cycle. When the water comes to a full boil, you are ready to begin.

5. Lay the cloth or a double or triple layer of cheesecloth in the steamer basket or tray. Pour the rice onto the cloth and spread it out as evenly as possible. Make a shallow depression 2 inches in diameter in the center of the rice. This allows the steam to circulate and cook the rice evenly. Fold the corners of the cloth over the rice to cover it completely. Place the steamer basket in the rice cooker and close the cover. Set a timer for 40 minutes. After 15 minutes of cooking, open the cover, taking care to avoid steam burns, and fold back the cloth. Sprinkle ⅓ cup (80 ml) water over the rice. Re-cover the rice with the cloth, close the cover, and proceed with the steaming. Repeat the water-sprinkling process once or twice during the cooking. When the timer sounds, open the cover and taste some rice. It should be tender. If it's not, or if you are not sure, let the rice steam for 10 minutes more.

6. Transfer the cooked rice to a large bowl and fan it to cool the rice quickly.

7. Serve the rice immediately or, if you are making it ahead of time, cover it with a clean, dry tea towel and store it at cool room temperature. (If you have made the rice a day ahead, refrigerate it, tightly covered.) You can reheat sticky rice in the steamer or microwave oven.

Long- or Medium-Grain Brown Rice

▸ MACHINE: Medium (6-cup [1.4 L]) rice cooker; fuzzy logic or on/off ▸ CYCLE: Regular ▸ YIELD: Serves 4

There are lots of long-grain brown rices, most sold in generic-looking bags. They come in a range of natural colors, from creamy to dark tan, with a flavor palate to match. We find long-grain brown rice has its own special sweetness, a far different flavor from medium- or short-grain. Brown rice takes more water and a longer time to cook than white rice, so plan your meal accordingly. You will use this same proportion scale for medium-grain brown rice.

> 1 cup (185 g) domestic long-grain brown rice
> 2 cups (475 ml) plus 1 tablespoon (15 ml) water

1. Place the rice in a fine strainer or bowl, rinse with cold water until the water runs clear, and drain.

2. Place the rice in the rice cooker bowl. Add the water, swirl to combine, close the cover, and set for the Regular cycle.

3. When the machine switches to the Keep Warm cycle, let the rice steam for 10 to 15 minutes. Fluff the rice with a wooden or plastic rice paddle or wooden spoon. This rice will hold on Keep Warm for 1 to 2 hours. Serve hot.

Short-Grain Brown Rice

▸ MACHINE: Medium (6-cup [1.4 L]) rice cooker; fuzzy logic or on/off ▸ CYCLE: Brown Rice or Regular ▸ YIELD: Serves 4

Short-grain brown rice is beloved by vegetarians, health food advocates, macrobiotics, Somersizers, and everyone else who loves chewy, flavorful brown rice. Short-grain brown rice is not as smoothly sweet as long-grain and makes a perfect side dish with a bit of butter or *gomasio* (page 69), a sesame salt condiment very popular in Japanese cuisine. If you want a brown rice risotto (don't tell the purists) or a dessert pudding, this would be the rice to use.

> 1 cup (180 g) short-grain brown rice
> 2¼ cups (535 ml) cold water

1. Place the rice in a fine strainer or bowl, rinse with cold water until the water runs clear, and drain.

2. Place the rice in the rice cooker bowl. Add the water; swirl to combine. If you have the time, soak the rice in its cooking water for 30 minutes to 1 hour. Close the cover and set for the Brown Rice or Regular cycle.

3. When the machine switches to the Keep Warm cycle, let the rice steam for 10 to 15 minutes. Fluff the rice with a wooden or plastic rice paddle or wooden spoon. This rice will hold on Keep Warm for 1 to 2 hours. Serve hot.

Germinated Brown Rice

▸ MACHINE: Small (4-cup), medium (6-cup [1.4 L]), or large (10-cup) rice cooker; fuzzy logic or on/off ▸ CYCLE: GABA or Regular ▸ YIELD: Serves 3 to 4

Germinated brown rice (GABA) is soaked in warm water long enough for germination to begin; the rice is then completely dried and packaged. Its appearance is no different than that of regular rice—there is no sprout to be seen and it is not soft or precooked. Germinated brown rice is believed to have additional health benefits, which are still being researched by scientists. Meanwhile, our kitchen research has determined that germinated brown rice has a delicious, nutty flavor and a slightly chewy texture. If you find regular brown rice too mushy, give germinated brown rice a try.

1 cup (180 g) germinated brown rice
1¾ cups (410 ml) water

1. Place the rice in the rice cooker bowl. Add the water; swirl to combine. Close the cover and set for the GABA or Regular cycle.

2. When the machine switches to the Keep Warm cycle, let the rice steam for 15 minutes. Fluff the rice with a wooden or plastic rice paddle or wooden spoon. This rice will hold for 2 to 3 hours on Keep Warm. Serve hot.

Brown Basmati Rice

▸ MACHINE: Medium (6-cup [1.4 L]) rice cooker; fuzzy logic or on/off ▸ CYCLE: Regular ▸ YIELD: Serves 4

Considering how aromatic white basmati rice is, you will have a shock if you expect the imported brown unhulled basmati to taste and smell the same. It doesn't. It might as well be an entirely different rice. First, the dark tan rice is a lot less foamy while washing. The aroma is distinctly grassy and the flavor delicately nutty. It takes fully twice the amount of time to cook as the white long-grain basmati. You can also use these proportions for the domestic brown basmati developed by Lundberg, which is a delicious, milder rice all around.

1 cup (180 g) imported Indian brown basmati rice
2 cups (475 ml) water
1 tablespoon (14 g) unsalted butter
¼ teaspoon salt

1. Place the rice in a fine strainer or bowl, rinse with cold water until the water runs clear, and drain.

2. Coat the rice cooker bowl with nonstick cooking spray or a film of vegetable oil. Place the rice in the rice bowl. Add the water, butter, and salt; swirl to combine.

3. Close the cover and set for the Regular cycle.

4. When the machine switches to the Keep Warm cycle, let the rice steam for 10 minutes. Fluff the rice with a wooden or plastic rice paddle or wooden spoon. This rice will hold on Keep Warm for 1 to 2 hours. Serve hot.

Wehani Rice

▶ MACHINE: Medium (6-cup [1.4 L]) rice cooker; fuzzy logic or on/off ▶ CYCLE: Regular ▶ YIELD: Serves 4

Wehani rice, which is a russet color and somewhere between a long- and medium-grain brown rice, is a specialty rice developed by the Lundberg brothers in the upper Sacramento delta in central California. This rice is served as the house rice at one of our local gourmet restaurants, with everything from grilled seafood to game hens. Let the rice sit for 15 minutes longer if it is too moist. You don't want a big clump of rice, but know that it tends to look moist, even if it will be delicate on the tongue. Don't add salt while Wehani is cooking; it will toughen the grain. This rice is delicious and one of our favorites in the brown rice genre (try it as a fried rice).

1 cup (180 g) Wehani rice
1¾ cups (410 ml) plus 2 tablespoons (28 ml) water
1 tablespoon (14 g) unsalted butter (optional)

1. Coat the rice cooker bowl with nonstick cooking spray or a film of vegetable oil. Place the rice in the rice bowl. Add the water and butter, if using, swirl to combine, close the cover, and set for the Regular cycle.

2. When the machine switches to the Keep Warm cycle, open and dry the inside of the cover. Crumple a clean paper towel and place it over the surface of the rice to absorb excess moisture. Close the cover and let the rice steam for 15 minutes. Remove the paper towel. Fluff the rice with a wooden or plastic rice paddle or wooden spoon. This rice will hold on Keep Warm for 1 to 2 hours. Serve hot.

Black Rice

▶ MACHINE: Medium (6-cup [1.4 L]) rice cooker; fuzzy logic or on/off ▶ CYCLE: Brown Rice or Regular ▶ YIELD: Serves 4

Forbidden Rice is a Chinese black rice. This rice is unusual because black rice is usually sticky; Forbidden Rice is not. It is known as having medicinal qualities. Because it still has its colorful bran layer, it turns an intriguing purple-black color when cooked. It is a sweet, rather moist rice with an ever so slight crunch and is perfectly addicting.

Note: This rice will stain the sides of your mouth for a short while, just like blueberries. Serve under stir-fries and with grilled poultry.

1 cup (180 g) Forbidden Rice (Chinese black rice)
1¾ cups (410 ml) water
¼ teaspoon salt (optional)

1. Place the rice in a fine strainer or bowl, rinse with cold water until the water runs clear, and drain. The water will turn grayish.

2. Coat the rice cooker bowl with nonstick cooking spray or a film of vegetable oil. Place the rice in the rice bowl. Add the water and salt, if using; swirl to combine. Close the cover and set for the Brown Rice or Regular cycle.

3. When the machine switches to the Keep Warm cycle, open and dry the inside of the cover. Crumple a clean paper towel and place it over the rice to absorb excess moisture. Close the cover and let the rice steam for 15 minutes. Remove the paper towel. Fluff the rice with a wooden or plastic rice paddle or wooden spoon. This rice will hold on Keep Warm for 1 to 2 hours. Serve hot.

SIMPLE RICES and SMALL MEALS

Saffron Rice — 54

Lemon Rice — 54

Asian Multigrain Rice — 55

Julia's Aromatic Basmati Rice — 56

Brown Rice with Miso — 56

Moroccan Brown Rice — 57

Greek Lemon and Dill Rice with Feta — 59

Brown Basmati Almondine (Julie's "Cheater Pilaf") — 60

Sweet Brown Rice with Curry, Carrots, and Raisins — 61

One-Pot Rice and Lentils, Indian Style — 62

Wehani Rice with Garden Vegetables — 63

Baby Artichokes and Arborio Rice — 64

Rice with Fresh Greens for a Crowd — 66

Mexican Rice and Beans — 67

Indonesian Rice Bowl — 69

Chicken Donburi — 70

Saffron Rice

▶ MACHINE: Medium (6-cup) rice cooker; fuzzy logic or on/off ▶ CYCLE: Regular ▶ YIELD: Serves 3 to 4

Plain long-grain white rice with a pinch of saffron—the bright orange stigmas from the flowering bulb *Crocus sativus*—added to the cooking water is a favorite rice from the British Isles to Poland. The rice takes on a lovely pale yellow cast. Use a tiny pinch of powdered saffron or crush a stigma or two between your fingers. It is important that it is no more than a pinch; you want only the faintest hint of the pungent spice in the cooked rice. Serve with roast lemon chicken or pork loin with prunes.

1 cup (185 g) long-grain white rice, such as
   basmati, Texmati, or Carolina
1½ cups (355 ml) water
¼ teaspoon salt
Pinch of saffron

1. If using basmati, place the rice in a fine strainer or bowl, rinse with cold water until the water runs clear, and drain.

2. Coat the rice cooker bowl with nonstick cooking spray or a film of vegetable oil. Place the rice in the rice bowl. Add the water, salt, and saffron; swirl just to combine, close the cover, and set for the Regular cycle.

3. When the machine switches to the Keep Warm cycle, let the rice steam for 15 minutes. Fluff the rice with a wooden or plastic rice paddle or wooden spoon. This rice will hold for 2 to 3 hours on Keep Warm. Serve hot.

Lemon Rice

▶ MACHINE: Medium (6-cup) rice cooker; fuzzy logic or on/off ▶ CYCLE: Regular ▶ YIELD: Serves 3 to 4

Beth's mom makes this fresh-tasting rice to serve with chicken sautés and grilled prawns. It is a favorite.

1 cup (185 g) long-grain white rice, such as
   basmati or Carolina
1½ cups (355 ml) chicken stock
Pinch of salt
1 large clove of garlic, peeled
2 teaspoons grated lemon zest
2 tablespoons (28 g) unsalted butter
2 tablespoons (8 g) chopped fresh Italian parsley
   leaves

1. If using basmati rice, place the rice in a fine strainer or bowl, rinse with cold water until the water runs clear, and drain.

2. Place the rice in the rice cooker bowl. Add the stock and salt, stir just to combine, then place the garlic in the center on top of the rice. Close the cover and set for the Regular cycle.

3. When the machine switches to the Keep Warm cycle, add the lemon zest, butter, and parsley; stir to combine. Close the cover and let the rice steam for 10 minutes. Fluff the rice with a wooden or plastic rice paddle or wooden spoon. This rice will hold on Keep Warm for 1 to 2 hours. Before serving, remove the garlic and discard. Serve hot.

Asian Multigrain Rice

▶ MACHINE: Medium (6-cup) rice cooker; fuzzy logic or on/off   ▶ CYCLE: Regular   ▶ YIELD: Serves 4 to 6

In Chinese specialty markets you can find an easy-to-use, inexpensive, and delicious grain blend that adds a sweetish, nutty flavor, fiber, and nutrition to your plain rice. It also adds color; the cooked grain blend will be tinted a light lavender. Greenmax Fine Multi Grains are imported from Taiwan. Look in the rice section for a small plastic bag containing a wide variety of grains, including two kinds of barley, four kinds of rice, buckwheat groats, fox-nuts, whole millet, wheat, and oats. As you can imagine, this blend is quite assertively flavored. We like it best combined with regular white rice to mute the flavors. Be sure to soak the mixture for an hour before cooking to soften the whole grains.

1½ cups (300 g) or 2 rice cooker cups Japanese-style short- or medium-grain white rice

¾ cup (101 g) or 1 rice cooker cup multigrain blend

3¾ cups (875 ml) water

1. Wash the rice. Place the rice in a bowl (or use the bowl of your rice cooker) and fill the bowl about half-full with cold tap water. Swirl the rice in the water with your hand. Carefully pour off most of the water, holding one cupped hand under the stream to catch any grains of rice that are carried away with the water. Holding the bowl steady with one hand, use the other to rub and squeeze the wet rice, turning the bowl as you go, so that all the rice is "scrubbed." The small amount of water in the bowl will turn chalky white. Now, run cold water into the bowl, give the rice a quick swish, and carefully drain off the water as before. Repeat the scrubbing and pouring-off process two more times. By the third time, the water you pour off will be nearly clear.

2. Place the rice and multigrain blend in the rice cooker bowl. Add the water; swirl to combine. Let the grains soak for 1 hour.

3. Close the cover and set for the Regular cycle. When the machine switches to the Keep Warm cycle, let the grains steam for 15 minutes. Fluff the grains with a wooden or plastic rice paddle or wooden spoon. This rice will hold on Keep Warm for 1 to 2 hours. Serve hot.

Julia's Aromatic Basmati Rice

▶ MACHINE: Medium (6-cup [1.4 L]) rice cooker; fuzzy logic or on/off ▶ CYCLE: Regular ▶ YIELD: Serves 3

From excellent cook and friend Julia Scannel, here is a quick weeknight fluffy rice, which she learned when working on a book of recipes, *Cooking with the Spices of India* (Culinary Alchemy, 1995). The whole spices add a gentle scent and subtle flavor to the rice, especially apparent in the rice close to the spices. You will need to go to a specialty grocery to purchase the whole green cardamom pods, a member of the ginger family, which are different than the bleached white ones that are used in Scandinavian cuisine. The spices are left whole during serving, but are not eaten. Serve with yogurt-marinated tandoori chicken and chutney.

1 cup (180 g) white basmati rice
1½ cups (355 ml) water
¼ teaspoon salt
1 stick of cinnamon (4 inches, or 5 cm)
3 green cardamom pods

1. Place the rice in a fine strainer or bowl, rinse with cold water, and drain.

2. Place the rice, water, salt, and spices in the rice cooker bowl; swirl to combine. Close the cover and set for the Regular cycle.

3. When the machine switches to the Keep Warm cycle, let the rice steam for 15 minutes. Fluff the rice with a wooden or plastic rice paddle or wooden spoon. This rice will hold on Keep Warm for 3 to 4 hours. Serve hot.

Brown Rice with Miso

▶ MACHINE: Medium (6-cup [1.4 L]) rice cooker; fuzzy logic or on/off ▶ CYCLE: Brown Rice or Regular ▶ YIELD: Serves 3 to 4

Salty miso, a fermented soybean paste t, adds a nice, healthy dimension to plain brown rice (a little dab will do ya, as it is quite strongly flavored). The mildest misos are white or creamy yellow-white, suitable for this recipe (the darker the color of the miso, from red to brown, the stronger the flavor). This rice is really good alongside simple steamed or sautéed vegetables. You can use long-, medium-, or short-grain brown rice in this recipe. Top with minced fresh Italian parsley, mitsuba (a Japanese herb found fresh in Asian markets), or green onion tops, and some cubed hot or cold tofu.

1½ tablespoons (24 g) white or yellow miso
2¼ cups (535 ml) water or vegetable stock
1 piece of fresh ginger (1 inch, or 2.5 cm), peeled
Juice of ½ of a small lemon (about 2 teaspoons)
1 cup (185 g) brown rice

1. In a small bowl, mash the miso in ¼ cup (60 ml) of the water to dissolve.

2. Place the dissolved miso, the remaining 2 cups (475 ml) water, the ginger, and lemon juice in the rice cooker bowl. Add the rice; swirl to combine. Close the cover and set for the Brown Rice or Regular cycle.

3. When the machine switches to the Keep Warm cycle, let the rice steam for 15 minutes. Fluff the rice with a wooden or plastic rice paddle or wooden spoon. Remove and discard the ginger before serving. This rice will hold on Keep Warm for 1 to 2 hours. Serve hot.

Moroccan Brown Rice

▶ MACHINE: Medium (6-cup [1.4 L]) rice cooker; fuzzy logic or on/off ▶ CYCLE: Regular ▶ YIELD: Serves 4 to 5

As guests of the Oldways Food Preservation Society of Boston, a group of food writers and restaurateurs traveled en masse to Morocco a few years ago. The result was an epiphany regarding North African cuisine, so influenced by the French and Arabs, with the food-loving public reaping the benefit of many excellent articles, travelogues, and exceptional recipes from the little-known land of *Casablanca* fame.

While couscous is the most prevalent starch in Moroccan cuisine, rice is also made. Serve this slightly spiced rice with an array of plain, separately steamed vegetables—green beans, fava or lima beans, carrots, butternut squash, celery, zucchini—and some chickpeas. Preserved lemons are often available in Middle Eastern markets.

1½ cups (278 g) aromatic long-grain brown rice, such as Texmati
2¾ cups (650 ml) water or vegetable stock
¾ teaspoon salt
½ teaspoon freshly ground black pepper
1 teaspoon ground coriander
½ teaspoon ground cardamom
3 tablespoons (42 g) unsalted butter, cut into pieces
Minced preserved lemon, for garnish

1. Coat the rice cooker bowl with nonstick cooking spray or a film of vegetable oil. Place the rice in the rice bowl. Add the water, salt, pepper, coriander, and cardamom; swirl just to combine. Close the cover and set for the Regular cycle.

2. When the machine switches to the Keep Warm cycle, add the butter. Close the cover and let the rice steam for 10 minutes. Fluff the rice with a wooden or plastic rice paddle or wooden spoon. This rice will hold on Keep Warm for 2 hours. Serve hot, sprinkled with the preserved lemon.

Greek Lemon and Dill Rice with Feta

▶ MACHINE: Medium (6-cup [1.4 L]) rice cooker; fuzzy logic or on/off ▶ CYCLE: Regular ▶ YIELD: Serves 3 to 4

The Greeks have a culinary love affair with the mating of lemon and dill, two plants that have been used since antiquity (lemon trees were planted along the Tigris and Euphrates Rivers). Dill is native to the eastern Mediterranean and contains a flavor element called limonene, which is a natural flavor complement to lemon. In Greek cooking, you find this combination in everything from soups to meat dishes. Rice is no exception. The mint is an optional ingredient, but a traditional one. This dish is also good made with brown rice; if you use it, increase the amount of chicken stock to 2⅔ cups (635 ml).

1. Coat the rice cooker bowl with nonstick cooking spray or a film of olive oil. Place the rice in the rice bowl. Add the stock; swirl to combine. Close the cover and set for the Regular cycle.

2. When the machine switches to the Keep Warm cycle, let the rice steam for 10 minutes.

3. While the rice is steaming, in a small skillet, heat the olive oil over medium heat. Add the onions and cook, stirring, until translucent and softened, about 5 minutes. Add the pine nuts and cook, stirring constantly, until golden brown (it won't take long).

4. When the steaming period is finished, add the sautéed mixture to the rice bowl, along with the lemon juice, dill, and mint. Stir with a wooden or plastic rice paddle or wooden spoon to evenly distribute. Close the cover and let the rice steam for an additional 10 minutes on the Keep Warm cycle.

5. Serve the rice immediately, topped with some feta cheese and a lemon wedge on the side.

Note: This rice will hold on Keep Warm for 1 to 2 hours, if necessary, but don't add the lemon juice, dill, and mint until 10 minutes before you plan to serve.

1½ cups (278 g) long-grain white rice, such as basmati, Jasmati, Carolina, or jasmine

2 cups (475 ml) chicken stock

2 tablespoons (28 ml) olive oil

2 small white boiling onions, chopped

¼ cup (35 g) pine nuts

¼ cup (60 ml) fresh lemon juice

1 tablespoon (4 g) minced fresh dill or 1 teaspoon dillweed

1½ teaspoons minced fresh mint leaves or ½ teaspoon dried mint leaves, crumbled

1 cup (150 g) crumbled feta cheese

1 lemon, cut into 8 wedges

Brown Basmati Almondine (Julie's "Cheater's Pilaf")

▶ MACHINE: Small (4-cup) or medium (6-cup [1.4 L]) rice cooker; fuzzy logic or on/off ▶ CYCLE: Regular
▶ YIELD: Serves 3 to 4

¾ cup (135 g) brown basmati rice
1¾ cups (410 ml) water
1 tablespoon (14 g) ghee (clarified butter; or unsalted butter
3 tablespoons (21 g) slivered almonds
¼ teaspoon salt
⅛ to ¼ teaspoon ground allspice, to taste

Brown basmati rice presented us with a bit of a challenge. Raw, it has a distinctly grassy odor. If you don't cook it for long enough, the grassy odor and flavor will linger. The trick is to cook it in plenty of water, which ensures that you will be rewarded with fluffy, aromatic grains and a delicate, almost nutty flavor. This elegant side dish is just right with a lightly seasoned baked fish or plain roasted chicken. No one will be able to identify the hint of allspice.

1. Place the rice in a fine strainer or bowl, rinse with cold water, rubbing it with your hands to remove any bits of dust; drain. Repeat.

2. Place the rice in the rice cooker bowl. Add the water; swirl to combine. Close the cover and set for the Regular cycle.

3. When the machine switches to the Keep Warm cycle, let the rice steam for 15 minutes.

4. While the rice is steaming, prepare the almonds. Melt the ghee in a small skillet over medium heat. Add the almonds and cook, stirring a few times, until golden brown, 2 to 3 minutes. Watch carefully; they burn easily. Set aside.

5. When the steaming period is finished, fluff the rice with a wooden or plastic rice paddle or wooden spoon. This rice will hold on Keep Warm for 3 to 4 hours.

6. Just before serving, add the almonds, salt, and allspice to the rice; stir to evenly distribute. Serve immediately.

Sweet Brown Rice with Curry, Carrots, and Raisins

▶ MACHINE: Medium (6-cup [1.4 L]) rice cooker; fuzzy logic or on/off ▶ CYCLE: Regular ▶ YIELD: Serves 3 to 4

We adapted this recipe for a simple one-pot meal from one we found on a gluten-free website. The green curry paste provides a sumptuous counterpoint to the carrots and raisins, so don't skip it. Serve with a dollop of plain Greek yogurt and/or hummus on the side to offset the sweetness.

1. Place the rice, carrot, and raisins in the rice cooker bowl. Add the water and apple juice, then the curry paste; swirl just to combine. Close the cover and set for the Regular cycle.

2. When the machine switches to the Keep Warm cycle, let the rice steam for 5 minutes. Gently fluff the rice with a wooden or plastic rice paddle or wooden spoon. Serve hot.

1 cup (185 g) long-grain brown rice or (180 g) brown jasmine rice
1 medium carrot, cut into matchsticks
¼ cup (35 g) golden raisins or (38 g) diced apple
2 cups (475 ml) water or vegetable broth
⅓ cup (80 ml) unsweetened apple juice
½ to 1 teaspoon mild or hot green curry paste

One-Pot Rice and Lentils, Indian Style

▶ MACHINE: Medium (6-cup [1.4 L]) rice cooker; fuzzy logic or on/off ▶ CYCLE: Regular ▶ YIELD: Serves 2 to 3

1 cup (180 g) white or
brown basmati rice
⅔ cup (139 g) mung dal,
picked over
2⅓ cups (555 ml) water or
vegetable broth
2 tablespoons (28 ml) olive
oil
Pinch of turmeric
¼ teaspoon ground cumin,
or to taste (or cumin
seeds crushed in a
mortar and pestle)
1 piece of fresh ginger
(1 inch, or 5 cm), peeled
and grated (1 to
2 teaspoons)
½ of a ripe tomato or
1 medium Roma plum
tomato, seeded and
chopped
1 cup (weight will vary)
mixed chopped fresh or
frozen thawed vegetables,
or 1 handful of baby
spinach leaves, rinsed
Pinch of red pepper flakes,
1 jalapeño chile (just lay
the whole chile in the
pot), or 1 to 2 teaspoons
minced canned chipotle
chiles in adobo sauce
(optional)
Salt
Freshly ground black
pepper
⅓ cup (5 g) packed fresh
cilantro leaves, chopped

While we are becoming more accustomed to the rejuvenating breakfast porridges and savory soups like Indian *kitchari,* there is also a *kitchari* that is dry like a pilaf with similar ingredients. Basmati rice and the quick-cooking yellow mung dal (split hulled green mung beans) are the primary ingredients for this dish. Individual cooks use their own proportions of rice to dal, but in this version we are doubling the amount of rice usually used to create a dish more like a pilaf. If you like, you can substitute yellow split peas for the *mung* (a combination of the *mung* and split peas or red lentils is good, too). This is delicious hot from the cooker, or cold carried for lunch the next day. Top it with a dollop of plain Greek yogurt or chopped cashews, or serve with a slice of baked tofu on the side.

1. Place the rice and dal in a fine strainer or bowl, rinse with cold water until the water runs clear, and drain.

2. Place the rice and dal in the rice cooker bowl. Add the water, oil, turmeric, cumin, ginger, tomato, vegetables, and red pepper, if using. Stir to distribute. Close the cover and set for the Regular cycle.

3. When the machine switches to the Keep Warm cycle, let the rice steam for at least 10 to 15 minutes. Taste for salt and pepper. Sprinkle with the cilantro. Serve immediately while hot, or let stand, covered, on the counter and eat later at room temperature.

Wehani Rice with Garden Vegetables

▶ MACHINE: Medium (6-cup [1.4 L]) rice cooker; fuzzy logic or on/off ▶ CYCLE: Regular ▶ YIELD: Serves 2 to 3

The Lundberg family has been breeding and growing aromatic and organic rices for years in northern California. A favorite is the aromatic Wehani rice bred by the Lundbergs themselves. It packs such a wallop of flavor that it needs little embellishment. This recipe is from food and wine writer Lynn Alley, who leaves the rice cooking while she works in her garden. Then she tops it with young, fresh-picked veggies and a dusting of Parmesan. In the springtime, use peas, green onions, and fresh parsley from your garden, produce stand, or local farmers' market; in the summer, use tiny baby zucchini, slender green beans, and strips of red or yellow pepper. And in the fall, try little florets of broccoli, purple potatoes, and baby carrots. Don't bother cutting up the small veggies, simply scrub and steam them whole. A little bit of experience will teach you when the rice is about 10 minutes away from being done; add the vegetables then.

1. Place the rice in a fine strainer or bowl, rinse with cold water, and drain.

2. Place the rice in the rice cooker bowl. Add the water and food base, if using; stir briefly. Close the cover and set for the Regular cycle. About 10 minutes before the rice is finished cooking, arrange the vegetables on top of the rice to steam.

3. When the machine switches to the Keep Warm cycle, let the rice steam for 10 minutes.

4. To serve, divide the rice and vegetables into portions, or stir the vegetables into the rice, if desired. Sprinkle with the cheese and serve immediately.

1 cup (180 g) Wehani rice

1¾ cups (410 ml) plus 2 tablespoons (28 ml) water

1 tablespoon (18 g) onion or mushroom food base (available in natural food stores; optional)

About 2 cups (weight will vary) fresh vegetables (choice depending on the season)

3 tablespoons (15 g) freshly grated Parmesan cheese

Baby Artichokes and Arborio Rice

▶ MACHINE: Medium (6-cup [1.4 L]) or large (10-cup) rice cooker; fuzzy logic or on/off ▶ CYCLE: Regular
▶ YIELD: Serves 4

Juice of 1 lemon
8 baby artichokes of equal size
2 cups (360 g) Arborio or other medium-grain (risotto-style) rice
¼ cup (½ stick, or 55 g) unsalted butter, cut into 8 pieces
2 medium-size shallots, minced
¼ cup (15 g) minced fresh Italian parsley leaves
3 cups (700 ml) chicken stock
½ teaspoon salt
Freshly ground black pepper
3 tablespoons (15 g) freshly grated Parmesan cheese, plus more for serving

In the Puglia area of Italy, rice is cooked "Spanish" style—that is, similar to paella. Called a *tiella*, after the round terra-cotta dish it is baked in, the rice is layered with vegetables. You can use other Italian medium-grain rices in this dish, such as the Argentinean-grown Carnaroli rice imported by Lotus Foods. We must admit we have substituted frozen artichoke hearts for the fresh when artichokes are out of season.

1. Fill a large bowl with cold water and pour the lemon juice into it. Prepare the artichokes by bending the outer leaves back and snapping them off until only the yellow inside leaves remain. You will remove more leaves than you think you should; this is okay. How many you remove will depend on the size and tenderness of each artichoke. Cut ½ inch (1.3 cm) off the top of each artichoke with a sharp paring knife and trim the bottoms flat. Cut each in half lengthwise. Place the artichokes in the lemon water as you work to prevent discoloration.

2. Place the rice in a fine strainer or bowl, rinse with cold water until the water runs clear, and drain.

3. Place the butter pieces evenly over the bottom of the rice cooker bowl. Sprinkle with the shallots, then cover with the rice, then the parsley. Arrange the artichoke halves on top, stem sides slightly down, pressing into the rice. Pour the stock over the layered ingredients. Close the cover and set for the Regular cycle.

4. When the machine switches to the Keep Warm cycle, stir in the salt, pepper to taste, and cheese. Close the cooker and let the rice steam for 10 minutes.

5. Serve immediately. Spoon the rice and vegetables onto serving plates and pass more cheese on the side.

Rice with Fresh Greens for a Crowd

▶ MACHINE: Large (10-cup) rice cooker; fuzzy logic or on/off ▶ CYCLE: Regular ▶ YIELD: Serves 20 to 24

6 cups (1.1 kg) long-grain white rice, such as basmati, Texmati, converted, or Carolina

7¾ cups (1.8 L) water

5 tablespoons (70 g) unsalted butter, cut into pieces

1¼ tablespoons salt

½ cup (20 g) chopped fresh Italian parsley leaves

½ cup (48 g) chopped fresh mint leaves

½ cup (20 g) chopped fresh basil leaves

This recipe is perfect for entertaining; the combination of parsley, mint, and basil is very Italian and ever so good with grilled fish and chicken. Remember that, whenever cooking rice to the full capacity of the cooker bowl, the rice on the bottom will be a bit squishy, so a thorough but gentle mixing after the steaming period is imperative.

1. Place the rice in a fine strainer or bowl, rinse with cold water until the water runs clear, and drain.

2. Coat the rice cooker bowl with nonstick cooking spray or a film of vegetable oil. Place the rice in the rice bowl. Add the water, butter, and salt; swirl just to combine. Close the cover and set for the Regular cycle.

3. When the machine switches to the Keep Warm cycle, let the rice steam for 15 minutes. Add the herbs to the rice bowl; stir with a wooden or plastic rice paddle or wooden spoon to evenly distribute. Close the cover and let the rice steam for 30 minutes. This rice will hold on Keep Warm for up to 2 hours. Serve hot.

Mexican Rice and Beans

▶ MACHINE: Medium (6-cup [1.4 L]) rice cooker; fuzzy logic or on/off ▶ CYCLE: Regular ▶ YIELD: Serves 4

Rice and beans are partners in all ethnic cuisines—rice and lentils in India, sticky rice and red adzuki beans in Japan, rice and black beans in Cuba. Here, rice, pinto beans, chile peppers, and tomatoes, staples in the Mexican kitchen, are combined for a very simple all-in-one meal. Serve with warm corn tortillas. If you have an avocado tree or can find avocado leaves in a Mexican market, give that option a try.

1. Coat the rice cooker bowl with nonstick cooking spray or a film of vegetable oil. Add the rice, stock, and salt; swirl to combine. Close the cover and set for the Regular cycle.

2. While the rice is cooking, heat the olive oil in a large skillet over medium heat. Add the onion and bell pepper and cook, stirring, until softened, about 5 minutes. Open the cover of the rice cooker and add the jalapeño, onion-pepper mixture, pinto beans, tomatoes, oregano, capers, and a few grinds of black pepper; stir to combine. Close the cover and let the cycle complete.

3. When the machine switches to the Keep Warm cycle, let the rice steam for 10 minutes. Fluff the rice with a wooden or plastic rice paddle or wooden spoon. This rice will hold on Keep Warm for up to 1 hour.

4. Serve hot, garnished with the cilantro, crème fraîche, and crumbled cheese.

1 cup (185 g) long-grain white rice
1 cup (235 ml) chicken stock
Pinch of salt
1 tablespoon (15 ml) olive oil, vegetable oil, or rendered chicken fat
1 large yellow onion, chopped
1 red bell pepper, cored, seeded, and sliced
1 jalapeño chile, seeded and minced
1 can (15 ounces, or 425 g) of pinto beans, drained and rinsed
1 can (15 ounces, or 425 g) of can plum tomatoes (can be flavored with Mexican spices), with their juices
1 teaspoon crumbled dried oregano leaves or 1 small avocado leaf, toasted and crumbled
2 tablespoons (18 g) capers, rinsed
Freshly ground black pepper
3 tablespoons (3 g) chopped fresh cilantro leaves, for garnish
½ cup (112 g) crème fraîche, *crema Mexicana*, or (115 g) sour cream, for garnish
⅔ cup (100 g) crumbled *queso fresco* (available in the dairy section in supermarkets) or feta cheese, for garnish

Indonesian Rice Bowl

▶ MACHINE: Medium (6-cup [1.4 L]) rice cooker; fuzzy logic or on/off ▶ CYCLE: Regular ▶ YIELD: Serves 4

From one of the Bay Area's favorite food writers, backyard gardeners, and seed purveyors, Renee Shepherd, comes this satisfying one-dish meal adapted from her book *Recipes from a Kitchen Garden* (Ten Speed, 1993). This is a great recipe to use up leftover chicken. The popular peanut sauce is one of the definitive tastes of the Southeast Asian and Thai cuisines. This simplified version of the *rijsttafel* table, a popular full-rice meal in Indonesia, looks incredibly festive served with all the condiments.

1. Make the rice: Coat the rice cooker bowl with nonstick cooking spray or a film of vegetable oil. Place the rice in the rice bowl. Add the water; swirl to combine. Close the cover and set for the Regular cycle.

2. Make the sauce: In a medium-size saucepan, combine all the sauce ingredients. Cook over low heat, stirring a few times, until the mixture achieves a saucelike consistency. Cover and keep warm.

3. When the machine switches to the Keep Warm cycle, sprinkle the peas and chicken on top of the rice. Close the cover and let the rice steam for 20 minutes.

4. Transfer the rice mixture to a warmed serving platter with sloped sides. Pour the hot stock and peanut sauce over the rice. Stir gently to combine the peas and chicken with the stock and peanut sauce. Sprinkle with the green onion tops and peanuts. Serve immediately with a choice of condiments.

1 cup (180 g) Thai jasmine rice

1 cup (235 ml) plus 2 tablespoons (28 ml) water

2½ cups (375 g) fresh or (325 g) frozen petite peas (2 pounds [900 g] fresh unshelled)

2½ cups (313 g) shredded poached chicken breast

½ cup (120 ml) hot chicken stock

SAUCE

⅓ cup (87 g) creamy peanut butter

½ cup (120 ml) chicken broth or water

1 tablespoon (15 ml) dry sherry

2 tablespoons (28 ml) rice vinegar

2 teaspoons peeled and grated fresh ginger

⅛ teaspoon cayenne pepper

½ teaspoon sugar

1 clove of garlic, minced

2 green onions, white parts only, minced (chop the green tops for garnish)

½ cup (75 g) chopped roasted peanuts, for garnish

CONDIMENTS

Separate small bowls of chutney, sliced bananas, raisins, unsweetened shredded coconut, minced fresh cilantro leaves, mandarin orange segments, chopped apples, plain yogurt

Chicken Donburi

▶ MACHINE: Medium (6-cup [1.4 L]) rice cooker; fuzzy logic or on/off ▶ CYCLE: Regular ▶ YIELD: Serves 3

2 dried shiitake mushrooms (optional)

1½ cups (300 g) or 2 rice cooker cups Japanese-style short- or medium-grain white rice (not Arborio or other risotto-style rice)

2 cups (475 ml) water (1⅔ cups [395 ml] for short-grain rice)

Pinch of sea salt

2 cups (475 ml) Vegetarian Dashi (page 105) or chicken stock

3 tablespoons (45 ml) tamari soy sauce

3 tablespoons (45 ml) mirin (sweet rice wine), or 3 tablespoons (45 ml) sake and a pinch of sugar

3 boneless, skinless chicken thighs, trimmed of fat and cut into 1-inch (2.5 cm) strips

6 to 8 ounces (170 to 225 g) firm tofu, cut into cubes

Chopped green parts of green onions or minced fresh chives, for garnish

2 to 3 tablespoons (10 to 15 g) toasted Japanese sesame seeds (page 45), for garnish

Donburi is a Japanese dish that is served in a special oversized rice bowl of the same name. Once Beth discovered how much she loved Calrose and Tamaki Gold rices, she had to have a special but simple little meal with which to eat them. Here is one of her best and fastest. If you use the chicken stock, you can add a small piece of dried kombu seaweed (cut a 1-inch-square [2.5 cm] piece with kitchen shears), if you like. Mirin is a low-alcohol sweet cooking wine (of which there is also a nonalcoholic version available) that you can find in the Asian food section of the supermarket.

1. Place the mushrooms, if using, in a small bowl, cover with hot water, and soak for 30 minutes. Or partially cover the bowl with plastic wrap and microwave on HIGH power for 2 minutes. Drain the mushrooms, remove the stems, and cut the caps into thin slices.

2. Wash the rice. Place the rice in a bowl (or use the bowl of your rice cooker) and fill the bowl about half-full with cold tap water. Swirl the rice in the water with your hand. Carefully pour off most of the water, holding one cupped hand under the stream to catch any grains of rice that are carried away with the water. Holding the bowl steady with one hand, use the other to rub and squeeze the wet rice, turning the bowl as you go, so that all the rice is "scrubbed." The small amount of water in the bowl will turn chalky white. Now, run cold water into the bowl, give the rice a quick swish, and carefully drain off the water as before. Repeat the scrubbing and pouring-off process two more times. By the third time, the water you pour off will be nearly clear.

3. Place the rice in the rice cooker bowl. Add the water and salt; swirl to combine. Close the cover and let the rice soak for 30 minutes to 1 hour. When the soaking period is finished, set for the Regular cycle.

4. When the machine switches to the Keep Warm cycle, let the rice steam for 15 minutes. Fluff the rice gently but thoroughly with a wooden or plastic rice paddle or wooden spoon. Close the cover and let the rice steam for another 10 to 15 minutes.

5. Meanwhile, poach the chicken. In a medium-size saucepan, combine the dashi, tamari, and mirin. Bring to a simmer over medium heat. Add the chicken and mushrooms, if using, and cook, partially covered, until the chicken is cooked through, 5 to 7 minutes. At the very end, toss in the tofu and let it heat for a minute or so.

6. When the rice has finished steaming, fluff it with the paddle or spoon again. Spoon the rice into individual bowls and top each with a portion of the chicken and tofu mixture. Ladle some of the poaching broth over the top and garnish with the green onions and sesame seeds. Serve immediately.

PILAFS

Riz au Beurre — 73

Qui's Basmati Pilaf — 73

Brown Rice Pilaf — 74

Indian Yellow Rice — 75

Tomato-Rice Pilaf — 75

Rice Pilaf with Fresh Peas — 77

Carrot Basmati — 78

Mexican Rice — 79

Arroz Verde — 80

Thai Curried Rice — 81

Rice Cooker Paella — 82

Vegetable Paella — 84

Arroz con Pollo — 85

A pilaf, so to speak, is as old as the hills. Invented in ancient Persia, it is derived from the Turkish word *pilau*, the method of preparing rice by first cooking it in meat fat or oil to enrich the flavor and keep the grains perfectly separated when cooked, then adding meat or poultry broth for steaming.

Riz au Beurre

▶ MACHINE: Medium (6-cup [1.4 L]) rice cooker; fuzzy logic or on/off ▶ CYCLE: Quick Cook and/or Regular ▶ YIELD: Serves 6 to 8

This is an incredibly easy pilaf. The rice, which must be just plain old long-grain (not jasmine), is sautéed in butter before cooking. If you use converted rice, a Parisian home favorite, be sure to increase the amount of water. A bit more butter is stirred in at serving time and, *voilà!*

> 4½ tablespoons (65 g) unsalted butter
> 2 cups (370 g) long-grain white rice, such as Carolina or Texmati
> 2¾ cups (650 ml) water
> 1 teaspoon salt (¾ teaspoon if using salted butter)
> Freshly ground black pepper (optional)
> Soy sauce (optional)

1. Set the rice cooker for the Quick Cook or Regular cycle. Place 2½ tablespoons (35 g) of the butter in the rice cooker bowl. When melted, add the rice. Cook, stirring a few times, until all the grains are evenly coated and hot, about 10 minutes. Add the water and salt; stir just to combine. Close the cover and reset for the Regular cycle or let the Regular cycle complete.

2. When the machine switches to the Keep Warm cycle, open the cover and dot the top of the rice with the remaining 2 tablespoons (28 g) butter, cut into pieces. Close the cover and let the rice steam for 15 minutes. Fluff the rice with a wooden or plastic rice paddle or wooden spoon. This pilaf will hold on Keep Warm for 2 to 3 hours. Serve hot, passing the pepper grinder or a cruet of soy sauce.

Qui's Basmati Pilaf

▶ MACHINE: Medium (6-cup [1.4 L]) rice cooker; fuzzy logic or on/off ▶ CYCLE: Quick Cook and/or Regular ▶ YIELD: Serves 3

Qui was a Vedantic nun in the early 1960s when she learned the intricacies of cooking basmati rice, a favorite in the ashram kitchen, but unheard-of in American homes at the time. One of her special preparations when she visits Beth is this rice served with yellow split pea soup poured over it and long pieces of curved butter-fried banana halves on the side.

> 1 cup (180 g) white basmati rice
> 2 tablespoons (28 g) unsalted butter
> 1½ cups (355 ml) water
> ¼ teaspoon fine sea salt

1. Place the rice in a fine strainer or bowl, rinse with cold water two to four times, and drain. The water will be chalky and slightly foamy. Spread the wet rice out with your hands on a clean tea towel on the counter. Let the rice air-dry for at least 1 hour, until cooking time (optional).

2. Set the rice cooker for the Quick Cook or Regular cycle. Place the butter in the rice cooker bowl. When melted, add the rice. Cook, stirring a few times, until all the grains are evenly coated, just ever-so-slightly golden, and hot, 10 to 15 minutes. Add the water and salt; stir just to combine. Close the cover and reset for the Regular cycle or let the Regular cycle complete.

3. When the machine switches to the Keep Warm cycle, let the rice steam for 10 minutes. Fluff the rice with a wooden or plastic rice paddle or wooden spoon. This pilaf will hold on Keep Warm for 2 to 3 hours. Serve hot.

Brown Rice Pilaf

▸ MACHINE: Medium (6-cup [1.4 L]) rice cooker; fuzzy logic or on/off ▸ CYCLE: Quick Cook and/or Regular
▸ YIELD: Serves 4

2½ tablespoons (38 ml)
    extra-virgin olive oil
1 cup (185 g) long-grain
    brown rice
2¼ cups (535 ml) water
¼ teaspoon salt

BOUQUET GARNI
Few sprigs of fresh parsley
1 bay leaf
Few celery leaves
1 sprig of fresh thyme,
    savory, marjoram, or
    rosemary

Be sure to use long-grain brown rice in this recipe. We like to use organic, if possible, as the bran layers of brown rice can store the residue of any pesticides used in the growing. Keep your brown rice in the refrigerator, especially in the summer, as the good, nutritious oils can go rancid. We love to concoct the bouquet garni, especially nice if you have a small garden. If you don't, when you buy fresh herbs, air-dry some of the sprigs on a paper towel for a few days on the kitchen counter for later use in your herb bundles. The herbs and the olive oil cut the inherent sweetness of the rice perfectly.

1. Set the rice cooker for the Quick Cook or Regular cycle. Place the olive oil in the rice cooker bowl. When hot, add the rice. Cook, stirring a few times, until all the grains are evenly coated and hot, about 10 minutes.

2. While the rice is cooking, assemble the bouquet garni. Tie the herbs into a bundle using a piece of chive or kitchen twine. Place the bouquet garni on top of the rice. Add the water and salt; stir just to combine. Close the cover and reset for the Regular cycle or let the Regular cycle complete.

3. When the machine switches to the Keep Warm cycle, remove the bouquet garni and discard it. Close the cover and let the rice steam for 10 minutes. Fluff the rice with a wooden or plastic rice paddle or wooden spoon. This pilaf will hold on Keep Warm for up to 2 hours. Serve hot.

Indian Yellow Rice

▶ MACHINE: Medium (6-cup [1.4 L]) rice cooker; fuzzy logic or on/off ▶ CYCLE: Quick Cook and/or Regular ▶ YIELD: Serves 6 to 8

Turmeric is a rhizome, like ginger, and is grown in tropical areas, including India, the Philippines, Indonesia, and Taiwan. No surprise, it is used for its pungent flavor and dark yellow color in the cuisines of those regions. It is essential to some Indian spice blends, but is able to stand on its own in this simple aromatic rice that is perfect served with stir-fried vegetables.

1 tablespoon (15 ml) olive oil
2 tablespoons (28 g) unsalted butter
2 cups (360 g) white basmati rice
2 teaspoons turmeric
2½ cups (570 ml) chicken stock
½ teaspoon salt

1. Set the rice cooker for the Quick Cook or Regular cycle. Place the oil and butter in the rice cooker bowl. When melted, add the rice and turmeric. Cook, stirring a few times, until the rice is shiny and hot, about 10 minutes. Add the stock and salt; stir just to combine. Close the cover and reset for the Regular cycle or let the Regular cycle complete.

2. When the machine switches to the Keep Warm cycle, let the rice steam for 10 minutes. Fluff with a wooden or plastic rice paddle or wooden spoon. This pilaf will hold on Keep Warm for 1 to 2 hours. Serve hot.

Tomato-Rice Pilaf

▶ MACHINE: Medium (6-cup [1.4 L]) rice cooker; fuzzy logic or on/off ▶ CYCLE: Quick Cook and/or Regular ▶ YIELD: Serves 6

Tomato pilaf made with canned tomatoes, called *riz et tomate* in France, is good with roast beef and veal. It is similar to a favorite dish made in the Greek Peloponnesus, *spanakorizo*, where it can have fresh spinach or sautéed leeks added in and cooked lightly with the rice. If you like pilaf with a bit more zing, add a few shots of Tabasco or your favorite south-of-the-border hot sauce with the cooking broth. Serve topped with cold sour cream and minced fresh chives or crumbled feta or goat cheese.

3 tablespoons (42 g) unsalted butter
2 cups (370 g) long-grain white rice
1 can (14 ounces, or 390 g) chopped tomatoes, with their juices (about 2 cups [360 g])
1¼ cups (285 ml) chicken stock or water
¾ teaspoon salt

1. Set the rice cooker for the Quick Cook or Regular cycle. Place the butter in the rice cooker bowl. When melted, add the rice. Cook, stirring a few times, until all the grains are evenly coated and hot, about 10 minutes. Add the tomatoes and their juices, stock, and salt; stir just to combine. Close the cover and reset for the Regular cycle or let the Regular cycle complete.

2. When the machine switches to the Keep Warm cycle, let the rice steam for 10 minutes. Fluff with a wooden or plastic rice paddle or wooden spoon. This pilaf will hold on Keep Warm for 1 to 2 hours. Serve hot.

Rice Pilaf with Fresh Peas

▶ MACHINE: Medium (6-cup [1.4 L]) rice cooker; fuzzy logic or on/off ▶ CYCLE: Quick Cook and/or Regular
▶ YIELD: Serves 3 to 4

Rice has a natural affinity for peas. Food writer Bert Greene once remarked that fresh peas in the pod will eventually be as rare and as expensive as truffles. With due respect, this wonderful recipe should be made exclusively when fresh peas hit the market; frozen peas just will not taste the same. This recipe is made with two different rices, to give the pilaf a firmer texture than if it was made with all medium-grain rice, which is stickier.

1. Set the rice cooker for the Quick Cook or Regular cycle. Place the butter in the rice cooker bowl. When melted, add the shallots and celery. Cook, stirring a few times, until softened, about 2 minutes. Add the stock, peas, salt, and rices; stir just to combine. Close the cover and reset for the Regular cycle or let the Regular cycle complete.

2. When the machine switches to the Keep Warm cycle, let the rice steam for 10 minutes. Fluff with a wooden or plastic rice paddle or wooden spoon. This pilaf will hold on Keep Warm for up to 1 hour. Serve hot.

1 tablespoon (14 g) unsalted butter

1 tablespoon (10 g) minced shallots

2 tablespoons (15 g) minced celery

1½ cups (355 ml) chicken stock

1 cup (150 g) fresh peas

½ teaspoon salt

½ cup (93 g) long-grain white rice

½ cup (90 g) Italian Arborio or California medium-grain rice

Carrot Basmati Pilaf

▶ MACHINE: Medium (6-cup [1.4 L]) rice cooker; fuzzy logic or on/off ▶ CYCLE: Quick Cook and/or Regular
▶ YIELD: Serves 4

1½ tablespoons (21 g) unsalted butter or ghee (clarified butter)

3 tablespoons (30 g) minced shallots

1 cup (180 g) white basmati rice

2 to 3 carrots, cut into thin strips or very coarsely grated

1½ cups (355 ml) chicken stock

¼ teaspoon ground cardamom

Pinch of red pepper flakes

Grated zest of 1 small orange

½ teaspoon honey

⅛ teaspoon salt

The distinctly orange root of the carrot has been a common ingredient in both Eastern and Western kitchens for centuries. It has been a cultivated vegetable for 2,000 years. This Indian-style rice is slightly sweet and ends up looking like it is studded with vibrant jewels, with the bits of carrot strewn throughout. Serve with simple roasted meats.

1. Set the rice cooker for the Quick Cook or Regular cycle. Place the butter in the rice cooker bowl. When melted, add the shallots. Cook, stirring a few times, until softened, about 2 minutes. Add the rice and carrots and cook, stirring a few times, until all the grains are evenly coated and hot and the carrots have softened slightly, about 10 minutes. Add the stock, cardamom, red pepper flakes, orange zest, honey, and salt; stir just to combine. Close the cover and reset for the Regular cycle or let the Regular cycle complete.

2. When the machine switches to the Keep Warm cycle, let the rice steam for 15 minutes. Fluff the rice with a wooden or plastic rice paddle or wooden spoon. This pilaf will hold on Keep Warm for up to 1 hour. Serve hot.

Mexican Rice

▶ MACHINE: Medium (6-cup [1.4 L]) rice cooker; fuzzy logic or on/off ▶ CYCLE: Quick Cook and/or Regular
▶ YIELD: Serves 4

Tomato-based Spanish rice, *arroz alla Mexicana,* is a real standard in every Mexican home or restaurant kitchen. There are as many recipes as there are cooks, so Beth went to Jacquie McMahan for advice. "Always fresh tomato," she chanted, "and not too much." She uses pure ground New Mexico chile for a kick; in lieu of that, you can use a mixed chili powder, which also includes cumin and a few other spices. In central Mexico, this rice would be served with a topping of finely diced potato, carrot, and peas that have been tossed in a bit of vinegar and oil.

1 tablespoon (15 ml) olive oil
⅓ cup (55 g) finely chopped onion
1 teaspoon minced garlic
1 cup (185 g) long-grain white rice, such as Texmati or Uncle Ben's converted
½ cup (90 g) peeled and chopped fresh tomato
1¾ cups (410 ml) water (2 cups [475 ml] for Uncle Ben's)
2 teaspoons pure ground chile or chili powder (We use Grandma's.)
½ teaspoon salt

1. Set the rice cooker for the Quick Cook or Regular cycle. Place the oil in the rice cooker bowl. When hot, add the onion and garlic. Cook, stirring a few times, until softened, about 2 minutes. Add the rice and cook, stirring a few times, until it turns ever-so-slightly golden, about 10 minutes. Add the tomato and sauté a bit longer. Add the water, chile, and salt; stir just to combine. Close the cover and reset for the Regular cycle or let the Regular cycle complete.

2. When the machine switches to the Keep Warm cycle, let the rice steam for 10 minutes. Fluff the rice with a wooden or plastic rice paddle or wooden spoon. This pilaf will hold on Keep Warm for 1 to 2 hours. Serve hot.

Arroz Verde

▶ MACHINE: Medium (6-cup [1.4 L]) rice cooker; fuzzy logic or on/off ▶ CYCLE: Quick Cook and/or Regular
▶ YIELD: Serves 4

2 cloves of garlic, peeled
½ cup (30 g) packed fresh Italian parsley leaves and small stems
½ cup (8 g) packed fresh cilantro leaves and small stems
1 cup (30 g) packed spinach leaves
2 cups (475 ml) chicken or vegetable stock
2 tablespoons (28 ml) vegetable oil
½ cup (80 g) finely chopped onion
1 cup (185 g) long-grain white rice
¼ teaspoon freshly ground black pepper, or to taste
Salt, if needed (omit if using canned broth)

Mexican cooks use their electric blenders frequently, for sauces, moles, and, here, to pulverize herbs and spinach in a flash. *Verde* means "green" in Spanish. Don't be intimidated by the amount of herbs called for; their flavor mellows substantially during cooking and creates a dish that's perfect alongside grilled chicken or fish or under a spicy stew.

1. Combine the garlic, parsley, cilantro, spinach, and 1 cup (235 ml) of the stock in a blender and process until smooth. Set aside.

2. Set the rice cooker for the Quick Cook or Regular cycle. Place the oil in the rice cooker bowl. When the oil is hot, add the onion. Cook, stirring a few times, until soft but not brown, about 5 minutes. Add the rice, stirring a few times, until all the grains are evenly coated and hot, about 10 minutes. Close the cover and allow the rice to cook, stirring a few times, until it smells toasty and begins to brown, about 5 minutes.

3. Add the herb and spinach puree, remaining 1 cup (235 ml) of stock, the pepper, and salt to taste, if using. Stir well with a wooden or plastic rice paddle or wooden spoon. Close the cover and reset for the Regular cycle or let the Regular cycle complete.

4. When the machine switches to the Keep Warm cycle, let the rice steam for 10 minutes. Stir well to incorporate the puree. This pilaf will hold on Keep Warm for up to 1 hour. Serve hot.

Thai Curried Rice

▶ MACHINE: Medium (6-cup [1.4 L]) rice cooker; fuzzy logic or on/off ▶ CYCLE: Quick Cook and/or Regular
▶ YIELD: Serves 4

This is a complex, spicy rice pilaf: It has spices, a bit of coconut milk, lime juice, soy sauce, ginger, raisins, almonds, and green onions. These recipe proportions are designed for American jasmine rice; if you use imported Thai jasmine rice or one of the colored jasmine rices, decrease the total liquid (some stock and some coconut milk) by ⅓ cup (80 ml). Serve with grilled or sautéed fish and poultry.

1. Preheat the oven to 325°F (170°C, or gas mark 3).

2. Set the rice cooker for the Quick Cook or Regular cycle. Place the butter in the rice cooker bowl. When melted, add the ginger and rice. Cook, stirring a few times, until the grains are evenly coated and hot, about 10 minutes. Add the curry powder and stir.

3. Meanwhile, in a large measuring cup, combine the stock, coconut milk, soy sauce, lime juice and zest, chile sauce, and salt. Add the stock mixture and raisins to the rice; stir just to combine. Close the cover and reset for the Regular cycle or let the Regular cycle complete.

4. While the rice is cooking, place the almonds on a baking sheet and bake until lightly toasted, about 6 minutes. Remove from the baking sheet and let cool to room temperature.

5. When the machine switches to the Keep Warm cycle, sprinkle the rice with the toasted almonds and green onions. Close the cover and let the rice steam for 15 minutes. Fluff the rice with a wooden or plastic rice paddle or wooden spoon. Serve immediately.

Note: This pilaf can be held for 1 to 2 hours on Keep Warm; however, do not add the almonds and green onions to the rice until 15 minutes before serving.

3 tablespoons (42 g) unsalted butter

1 tablespoon (6 g) peeled and minced fresh ginger

1 cup (180 g) domestic jasmine rice

1 tablespoon (6 g) mild or hot curry powder

1 cup (235 ml) plus 2 tablespoons (28 ml) chicken stock

⅓ cup (80 ml) canned unsweetened coconut milk (can be light)

2 tablespoons (28 ml) soy sauce

2 tablespoons (28 ml) fresh lime juice

Grated zest of 1 small lime

1 teaspoon Chinese hot chile sauce

Pinch of salt

⅓ cup (53 g) dark raisins, dried tart cherries, or (50 g) dried currants

⅓ cup (37 g) slivered blanched almonds

½ cup (50 g) minced green onions, both white and green parts

Rice Cooker Paella

▶ MACHINE: Large (10-cup) rice cooker; fuzzy logic or on/off ▶ CYCLE: Quick Cook and/or Regular
▶ YIELD: Serves 8

¼ cup (60 ml) extra-virgin olive oil
2 boneless, skinless chicken thighs, trimmed of fat and cut into ¾-inch (1.9 cm) pieces
1 medium-size onion, chopped
2 cloves of garlic, peeled
1 medium-size red bell pepper, seeded and cut into strips, the strips halved crosswise
1 cup (180 g) seeded and chopped fresh tomatoes
2 ounces (55 g) fully cooked smoked garlicky sausage (Spanish chorizo is traditional), sliced ⅓ inch (8 mm) thick
4 calamari, cleaned, bodies cut into ⅓-inch-wide (8 mm) rings, and each set of tentacles halved
3 cups (540 g) Arborio, Valencia, or other medium-grain white rice (not Japanese style)
5 cups (1.2 L) water
2 teaspoons salt
½ teaspoon freshly ground black pepper
½ teaspoon saffron threads
1 cup (100 g) fresh green beans, ends trimmed, cut into 1½-inch (3.8 cm) lengths
½ cup (65 g) small scallops
8 medium-size or large shrimp, shelled (tails left on) and deveined
½ cup frozen peas
8 small clams, washed in cold water to remove sand

You will need a large (10-cup) rice cooker to prepare paella for 8; halve the recipe for medium (6-cup [1.4 L]) machines. Don't be tempted to make this without the saffron; it is essential. You can order it (rather) reasonably from Penzeys, the spice merchants.

1. In a small nonstick skillet, heat 1 tablespoon (15 ml) of the olive oil over medium-high heat. When hot, add the chicken and cook, stirring, until just cooked through, 5 to 7 minutes. Remove the skillet from the heat.

2. Set the rice cooker for the Quick Cook or Regular cycle. Add the remaining 3 tablespoons (45 ml) of olive oil to the rice cooker bowl. When hot, add the onion. Cook, stirring a few times, until softened, about 2 minutes. Add the garlic, bell pepper, and tomatoes, stir to combine, and close the cover. Cook, stirring a few times, until the tomatoes break down and the bell pepper softens, about 10 minutes. Add the sausage, calamari, rice, chicken, water, salt, and black pepper; stir to combine. A pinch at a time, crumble the saffron threads into the rice bowl. Close the cover and reset for the Regular cycle or let the Regular cycle complete. When the liquid boils (open the cooker occasionally to check, if yours doesn't have a glass lid), add the green beans, stir quickly to combine, and close again.

3. When the machine switches to the Keep Warm cycle, be ready to act quickly. Open the cover, toss in the scallops, and quickly stir them into the rice mixture. Place the shrimp around the border of the rice cooker bowl, pressing them partway into the rice, so that their tails stick up. Sprinkle the peas over the entire surface of the rice. Nestle the clams about halfway into the rice, hinged sides down. Close the cover and let the paella steam until the clams open and the shrimp turn pink, about 15 minutes. Serve the paella immediately.

Note: If the clams do not open, perhaps there is not enough heat remaining in the rice cooker. Take them out and put them in a medium-size saucepan with about 1 inch (2.5 cm) of water. Cover the pot and bring the water to a boil. The clams should open in a few minutes. Throw out any that do not.

Vegetable Paella

▶ MACHINE: Medium (6-cup [1.4 L]) or large (10-cup) rice cooker; fuzzy logic or on/off
▶ CYCLE: Quick Cook and/or Regular ▶ YIELD: Serves 4

¼ cup (60 ml) olive oil
1 small dried red chile, broken
½ cup (90 g) diced onion
½ medium-size red bell pepper, halved, seeded, and sliced
½ medium-size green bell pepper, halved, seeded, and sliced
2 cloves of garlic, minced
1 teaspoon fresh oregano leaves, crushed between your fingers
1 teaspoon sweet or hot paprika
1 medium-size zucchini, cut into ½-inch (1.3 cm) cubes
2 large ripe tomatoes, peeled, seeded, and coarsely chopped
1¼ cups (225 g) Arborio, Valencia, or other medium-grain white rice (not Japanese style)
1¾ cups (410 ml) vegetable or chicken stock
Few saffron threads, crushed
1 teaspoon salt
Freshly ground black pepper
½ cup (75 g) fresh or (65 g) frozen petite peas

Here is an unorthodox, vegetarian, and much simplified version of the elaborate Spanish paella. It is an excellent side dish or vegetarian entrée.

1. Set the rice cooker for the Quick Cook or Regular cycle. Place the oil in the rice cooker bowl. When hot, add the chile, onion, and bell peppers. Cook, stirring a few times, until softened, about 10 minutes. Add the garlic, oregano, paprika, zucchini, and tomatoes. Close the cover and cook for 5 minutes. Stir in the rice, stock, and saffron. Add the salt and black pepper to taste; stir just to combine. Close the cover and reset for the Regular cycle or let the Regular cycle complete.

2. When the machine switches to the Keep Warm cycle, scatter the peas on top of the rice mixture. Close the cover and let the rice steam for 15 minutes. Fluff the rice with a wooden or plastic rice paddle or wooden spoon. This paella will hold on Keep Warm for up to 1 hour. Serve hot.

Arroz con Pollo

▶ MACHINE: Large (10-cup) rice cooker; fuzzy logic or on/off ▶ CYCLE: Quick Cook and/or Regular
▶ YIELD: Serves 4

1. Cut each chicken thigh in two. Place the chicken pieces on a plate and season them with half the lime juice and salt and pepper to taste. Let the chicken marinate for about 15 minutes.

2. In a heavy medium-size nonstick skillet, heat 1 tablespoon (15 ml) of the oil over high heat. When hot, brown the chicken pieces on both sides until golden, about 5 minutes per side. As they are browned, transfer them to a clean plate and set aside.

3. Set the rice cooker for the Quick Cook or Regular cycle. Heat the remaining 1 tablespoon (15 ml) oil in the rice cooker bowl. When hot, add the onion and garlic and stir to combine. Cook until the onion begins to soften, about 2 minutes. Do not allow the garlic to burn. Add the bell peppers; stir to combine. Add the rice and cumin; stir to combine and cook, stirring occasionally, until the rice is opaque, about 10 minutes.

4. Meanwhile, put the water in a 2-cup (475 ml) glass measuring cup. Add the remaining lime juice and the achiote paste, breaking up the achiote paste with your fingers as you add it (it can stain fabric, so take care). Stir to dissolve the achiote.

5. Add the cilantro and tomatoes to the rice cooker, along with 1 teaspoon salt and ½ teaspoon black pepper. Add the beer and achiote water. You'll need about ¾ cup (175 ml) additional liquid. If you have reserved tomato juices from the canned tomatoes, measure it, adding water to reach the ¾-cup (175 ml) level. If not, add an additional ¾ cup (175 ml) water. Stir well to combine the ingredients. Add the chicken, along with any juices that have accumulated on the plate. Push the chicken pieces down into the rice. Close the cover and reset for the Regular cycle or let the Regular cycle complete.

6. When the machine switches to the Keep Warm cycle, quickly open the cover and sprinkle the peas on top. Close the cover and let the rice steam for 10 to 15 minutes. Gently fluff the rice with a wooden or plastic rice paddle or wooden spoon and stir to incorporate the peas. Serve immediately.

---

4 boneless, skinless chicken thighs, trimmed of fat

Juice of 1 large or 2 small limes

Salt

Freshly ground black pepper

2 tablespoons (28 ml) olive or vegetable oil

1 medium-size onion, chopped

3 cloves garlic, minced

2 medium-size red bell peppers, seeded and cut into ½-inch (1.3 cm) squares

2 cups (370 g) long-grain white rice

½ teaspoon ground cumin

1 cup (235 ml) lukewarm water, plus more as needed

About 1 tablespoon (12 g) achiote paste (use less, 1 to 2 teaspoons, if you don't want a warmly spicy dish)

½ cup (8 g) chopped fresh cilantro leaves

1 cup (180 g) seeded and chopped fresh tomatoes (or use canned, reserving their juices)

1 bottle (12 ounces, or 355 ml) medium- or light-bodied beer

1 cup (130 g) frozen peas

RISOTTOS

Risotto Milanese — 87

Butternut Squash Risotto — 89

Dried Mushroom Risotto — 90

Asparagus and Mushroom Risotto — 91

Italian Sausage Risotto — 92

Risotto is part of the triumvirate of soul-satisfying Italian starches, along with polenta and pasta. It is described in literature as "gilded grains of gold," in reference to *risotto alla milanese*, where the cooked rice is bathed in a pale golden sheen of saffron. It is traditionally exclusively a first-course dish, a *primo piatto*, not an accompaniment like American rice, except when paired with osso bucco. Risotto is a unique type of rice dish with its very own consistency, which is likened to a sauce. Pearl-colored Arborio, the most well-known Italian rice for risotto, has a lot of surface starch, so the rice becomes creamy during cooking, almost like a savory rice pudding. Think of it cooking like pasta: tender on the outside and a hint of resistance on the inside. The center remains *al dente*, a very different culinary experience if you have never had it before; you might think your rice is not quite cooked.

Risotto Milanese

▶ MACHINE: Medium (6-cup [1.4 L]) or large (10-cup) rice cooker; fuzzy logic or on/off
▶ CYCLE: Quick Cook and/or Regular or Porridge   ▶ YIELD: Serves 4 to 5

Risotto Milanese, or risotto with saffron, is the national dish of the Lombardy region of Italy. It has been made there since the late eighteenth century as a special first course washed down with red wine. Use saffron threads here, as powdered saffron is really a lot more potent; you want a faint saffron flavor, not overpowering. It is traditionally served as a starchy side dish to osso bucco (braised veal shanks) and *carbonata* (Milanese beef stew).

1. In a small saucepan or in the microwave, heat 1 cup of the stock and crush the saffron into it; let stand for 15 minutes.

2. Set the rice cooker for the Quick Cook or Regular cycle. Place the olive oil and butter in the rice cooker bowl. When the butter melts, add the onion. Cook, stirring a few times, until softened, about 2 minutes. Stir in the wine and cook for 1 minute. Add the rice and stir occasionally until the grains are transparent except for a white spot on each, 3 to 5 minutes. Stir in the saffron stock and remaining 2 cups chicken stock. Close the cover and reset for the Porridge cycle, or for the Regular cycle and set a timer for 20 minutes.

3. When the machine switches to the Keep Warm cycle or the timer sounds, stir the rice with a wooden or plastic rice paddle or wooden spoon. The risotto should be only a bit liquid and the rice should be al dente, tender with just a touch of tooth resistance. If needed, cook for a few minutes longer. This risotto will hold on Keep Warm for up to 1 hour.

4. When ready to serve, add the butter. Close the cover for a minute to let the butter melt. Stir in the cheese and salt to taste. Serve immediately.

3 cups (700 ml) chicken stock, or 1 can (14.5 ounces, or 410 g) chicken broth plus water to equal 3 cups (700 ml)
Pinch of saffron threads
1 tablespoon (15 ml) olive oil
1 tablespoon (14 g) unsalted butter
¾ cup (120 g) finely chopped yellow onion
¼ cup (60 ml) dry white wine
1 cup (180 g) plus 2 tablespoons medium-grain risotto rice (*superfino* Arborio, Carnaroli, or Vialone nano)

TO FINISH
1 tablespoon (14 g) unsalted butter
¼ cup (25 g) freshly grated Parmesan cheese, plus more for serving
Salt

Butternut Squash Risotto

▸ MACHINE: Medium (6-cup [1.4 L]) or large (10-cup) rice cooker; fuzzy logic or on/off
▸ CYCLE: Quick Cook and/or Regular or Porridge   ▸ YIELD: Serves 4 to 5

This risotto is heavier on the vegetables (the winter squash and the onion) than is traditional, but it is a favorite autumn and winter variation. Use less squash if you like, but we feel the extra amount contributes a lovely flavor and color along with a nutritional boost. We also use half stock and half water in order not to overwhelm the delicate squash flavor. You can add some diced zucchini as well; it is a good flavor combination. We like the unconventional addition of lime juice; it brightens the flavor of the squash.

1. Set the rice cooker for the Quick Cook or Regular cycle. Place the olive oil and butter in the rice cooker bowl. When the butter melts, add the onion. Cook, stirring a few times, until softened, about 2 minutes. Add the rice and stir with a wooden or plastic rice paddle or wooden spoon to coat the grains with the hot butter. Cook, stirring a few times, until the grains of rice are transparent except for a white spot on each, 3 to 5 minutes. Add the squash, water, and stock; stir to combine. Close the cover and reset for the Porridge cycle, or for the Regular cycle and set a timer for 20 minutes.

2. When the machine switches to the Keep Warm cycle or the timer sounds, stir the risotto. It should be only a bit liquid, and the rice should be al dente, tender with just a touch of tooth resistance. If needed, cook for a few minutes longer. This risotto will hold on Keep Warm for up to 1 hour.

3. When ready to serve, add the butter. Close the cover for a minute to let the butter melt. Stir in the lime juice, parsley, cheese, and salt to taste. Serve immediately.

2 tablespoons (28 ml) olive oil
2 tablespoons (28 g) unsalted butter
⅔ cup (110 g) finely chopped yellow onion
1 cup (180 g) plus 2 tablespoons (23 g) medium-grain risotto rice (*superfino* Arborio, Carnaroli, or Vialone nano)
1¾ to 2 cups (245 to 280 g) peeled and seeded butternut squash cut into ½-inch (1.3 cm) cubes
1½ cups (355 ml) water
1½ cups (355 ml) chicken, veal, or vegetable stock

TO FINISH
2 teaspoons (28 g) unsalted butter
2 tablespoons (28 ml) fresh lime juice
¼ cup (15 g) minced fresh Italian parsley leaves
¼ cup (25 g) freshly grated Parmesan cheese, plus more for serving
Salt

Dried Mushroom Risotto

▶ MACHINE: Medium (6-cup [1.4 L]) or large (10-cup) rice cooker; fuzzy logic or on/off
▶ CYCLE: Quick Cook and/or Regular or Porridge ▶ YIELD: Serves 4 to 5

½ ounce (15 g) dried
mushrooms
1¾ cups (410 ml) hottest
possible tap water
About 1½ cups (355 ml)
beef, chicken, or vegeta-
ble stock
1 tablespoon (15 ml) olive
oil
1 tablespoon (14 g) unsalted butter
½ cup (90 g) minced onion
¼ cup (60 ml) dry white
wine
1 cup (180 g) plus 2
tablespoons (23 g) medi-
um-grain risotto rice (superfino Arborio, Carnaroli,
or Vialone nano)

TO FINISH
2 teaspoons unsalted but-
ter, or more, if desired
2 tablespoons (8 g)
chopped fresh Italian
parsley leaves
¼ cup (25 g) freshly grated
Parmesan cheese, plus
more for serving
Freshly ground black
pepper
Salt

* (If the mushrooms
were especially gritty,
you may want to pour
the liquid through a
coffee filter–lined
strainer, but in general
this is not necessary.)

If you like cream of mushroom soup, you will love this risotto, known as *risotto con funghi secchi*. Choose porcini, the Italian favorite, or another type of dried mushroom like morels, chanterelles, or shiitakes.

1. Place the mushrooms in a small bowl and add the hot water. Let stand for an hour or longer. (Or combine the mushrooms and water in a microwave-safe container, cover tightly with plastic wrap, and micro-wave on HIGH power for 5 minutes. Let cool to room temperature.) When the mushrooms are soft, remove them from the liquid, squeez-ing gently to extract as much liquid as possible. Slice the mushrooms into pieces about ¼ × 1 inch (6 mm × 2.5 cm), discarding any tough stems. The exact size is not important, but if you cut them too small, their flavor will not be as intense. Carefully pour the mushroom soak-ing liquid into a measuring cup, leaving any grit behind.* Add the stock to the mushroom soaking liquid to equal 3 cups (700 ml).

2. Set the rice cooker for the Quick Cook or Regular cycle. Place the olive oil and butter in the rice cooker bowl. When the butter melts, add the onion. Cook, stirring a few times, until softened, about 2 min-utes. Stir in the wine and cook for 1 to 2 minutes. Add the rice and stir until the grains are evenly coated and hot. Cook, stirring occasionally, until the grains are transparent except for a white spot on each, 3 to 5 minutes. Add the stock mixture and mushrooms to the rice; stir to combine. Close the cover and reset for the Porridge cycle, or for the Regular cycle and set a timer for 20 minutes.

3. When the machine switches to the Keep Warm cycle or the timer sounds, open the cover and stir with a wooden or plastic rice paddle or wooden spoon. The risotto should be only a bit liquid and the rice should be al dente, tender with just a touch of tooth resistance. If needed, cook for a few minutes longer. This risotto will hold on Keep Warm for up to 1 hour.

4. When ready to serve, add the butter. Close the cover for a minute to let the butter melt. Stir in the parsley, cheese, a few grinds of pep-per, and salt to taste. Serve immediately.

Asparagus and Mushroom Risotto

▶ MACHINE: Medium (6-cup [1.4 L]) or large (10-cup) rice cooker; fuzzy logic or on/off
▶ CYCLE: Quick Cook and/or Regular or Porridge   ▶ YIELD: Serves 4 to 6

This is the risotto Beth (and her mother) make *every* time they make risotto. The asparagus and mushrooms cook with the rice, so it is sort of a primavera (spring vegetable) stew. Asparagus risotto is one of the most popular variations after the saffron version. Vary this by substituting green beans, fresh peas, or zucchini for the asparagus, or combining any of them with it. This risotto is nice finished off with 2 tablespoons (28 ml) of heavy cream, if you happen to have any hanging around in the fridge.

1. Snap off the ends of the asparagus stalks and discard. If the remaining stalks are thick, peel with a vegetable peeler. Cut the spears on the diagonal into 2-inch (5 cm) pieces.

2. Set the rice cooker for the Quick Cook or Regular cycle. Place the olive oil and butter in the rice cooker bowl. When the butter melts, add the shallots. Cook, stirring a few times, until softened, about 2 minutes. Add the rice and stir until the grains are evenly coated and hot. Cook, stirring occasionally, until the grains are transparent except for a white spot on each, 3 to 5 minutes. Add the mushrooms and asparagus, stirring for a minute or two. Add the stock; stir to combine. Close the cover and reset for the Porridge cycle, or for the Regular cycle and set a timer for 20 minutes.

3. When the machine switches to the Keep Warm cycle or the timer sounds, stir the risotto with a wooden or plastic rice paddle or wooden spoon. The risotto should be only a bit liquid, and the rice should be al dente, tender with just a touch of tooth resistance. If needed, cook for a few minutes longer. This risotto will hold on Keep Warm for an hour or so.

4. When ready to serve, add the butter. Close the cover for a minute or so to allow the butter to melt. Stir in the cheese and salt to taste. Serve immediately.

¾ pound (340 g) fresh asparagus
1½ tablespoons (25 ml) olive oil
1½ tablespoons (21 g) unsalted butter
2 tablespoons (20 g) minced shallots
1 cup (180 g) plus 2 tablespoons (23 g) medium-grain risotto rice (*superfino* Arborio, Carnaroli, or Vialone nano)
2 ounces (55 g) fresh mushrooms, sliced
3 cups (700 ml) of chicken stock, or 1 can (14.5 ounces, or 410 g) of chicken broth plus water to equal 3 cups (700 ml)

TO FINISH
2 teaspoons unsalted butter
⅓ cup (33 g) freshly grated Parmesan cheese, plus more for serving
Salt

Italian Sausage Risotto

▸ MACHINE: Medium (6-cup [1.4 L]) or large (10-cup) rice cooker; fuzzy logic or on/off
▸ CYCLE: Quick Cook and/or Regular or Porridge ▸ YIELD: Serves 6 to 8

¾ pound (340 g) fennel or sweet Italian sausage, cut into ½-inch-thick (1.3 cm) slices

2 tablespoons (28 ml) water

2 tablespoons (28 ml) olive oil

2 tablespoons (28 g) unsalted butter

¼ cup (40 g) finely chopped yellow onion

½ cup (60 ml) dry white wine

2 cups (360 g) medium-grain risotto rice (*super-fino* Arborio, Carnaroli, or Vialone nano)

5 cups (1.2 L) of chicken stock, or 2 cans (14.5 ounces, or 410 g each) of chicken broth plus water to equal 5 cups (1.2 L)

TO FINISH
2 tablespoons (8 g) chopped fresh Italian parsley leaves

½ cup (50 g) freshly grated Parmesan cheese, plus more for serving

Salt

Freshly ground black pepper

This hearty winter risotto focuses its flavor on the spicy sausage, another Italian favorite. This recipe is a basic method and can be made with vegetables instead of sausage; substitute one to two diced roasted red or yellow bell peppers for the sausage. Note that this recipe is slightly larger than the others; it feeds six.

1. In a small skillet, combine the sausage and water. Cover and cook over medium-low heat until browned and heated through, about 5 minutes. Remove with a slotted spoon and drain on a double layer of paper towels.

2. Set the rice cooker for the Quick Cook or Regular cycle. Place the olive oil and butter in the rice cooker bowl. When the butter melts, add the onion. Cook, stirring a few times, until softened, about 2 minutes. Add the sausage and cook for a few minutes to heat it. Add the wine and cook until reduced, 1 to 2 minutes. Add the rice and stir to coat the grains with the hot butter. Cook, stirring occasionally, until the grains of rice are transparent except for a white spot on each, 3 to 5 minutes. Add the stock; stir to combine. Close the cover and reset for the Porridge cycle, or for the Regular cycle and set a timer for 25 minutes.

3. When the machine switches to the Keep Warm cycle or the timer sounds, stir the risotto with a wooden or plastic rice paddle or wooden spoon. The risotto should be only a bit liquid and the rice should be al dente, tender with just a touch of tooth resistance. If needed, cook for a few minutes longer. This risotto will hold on Keep Warm for an hour or so.

4. When ready to serve, stir in the parsley and cheese, season with salt and pepper to taste, and serve immediately.

SUSHI

Sushi Rice — 94

Maki Sushi — 97

California Rolls — 101

Chirashi Sushi (Osaka Style) — 102

Japanese home cooks make sushi often, but not the little fish-topped rice logs, called *nigiri sushi*, that are perhaps the most common sushi bar offerings. The word *sushi*, in fact, refers not to fish but to the vinegar-dressed rice that is the basis for a wide variety of sushi dishes. *Nigiri* sushi is deemed too hard to make at home. The sushi chef's special training is required for almost every step of the process—shaping the rice just so, cutting the fish properly, and so on. Home cooks have their own versions of sushi. Japanese home cooks prepare:

- *Maki* sushi—Seaweed-wrapped rolls that are sliced to expose the carefully arranged fillings inside.

- Hand rolls—The sushi rice is spread on a piece of seaweed, topped with fillings (you can use the fillings detailed below under the *maki* section), and casually rolled up in an ice-cream cone shape to be eaten out of hand.

- *Chirashi* sushi—This is like a rice salad, a sort of sushi in a bowl.

A Note About Storage
Some sushi, especially that containing raw fish, is eaten soon after it is made. But other types of sushi, especially the Osaka-style *chirashi* sushi on page 102, can be made hours ahead. Store in an airtight container at *cool* room temperature. Don't refrigerate unless absolutely necessary; the rice will harden.

Sushi Rice

▶ MACHINE: Medium (6-cup [1.4 L]) rice cooker; fuzzy logic or on/off   ▶ CYCLE: Regular or Sushi
▶ YIELD: 5½ cups (1 kg) loosely packed rice

For any form of sushi, the first step is the rice, which your rice cooker will allow you to prepare perfectly. Many rice cookers made for the Japanese market have a special Sushi cycle. Even if your cooker doesn't have this cycle, you can use it to make great sushi rice.

This is a basic recipe for rice cooker sushi rice. The amount of the vinegar dressing—and the manner in which it is seasoned with salt and sugar—is subject to both regional and personal variation. Sushi rice is said to be made saltier in the Tokyo area, sweeter near Osaka. Individual cooks vary the sugar and salt to suit their own tastes. The type of rice you use is very important; it will be labeled "short-grain" or "medium-grain" and you want a Japanese-style medium-grain rice, not a risotto or Carolina medium-grain rice. An excellent, but somewhat expensive, brand is Tamaki Gold from Williams Rice Milling Company of Williams, California. Other favorites that are good, and likely to be slightly cheaper, are Kokuho Rose and Nishiki. If you can't find them, look for rice labeled "new variety" or "sushi rice." Calrose is okay if you can't find anything else.

It is traditional to use a wooden bowl to mix your sushi rice because the wood absorbs excess moisture. This mixing tub is called a *han giri*, and it looks like half of a very flat wine barrel. It is made of a wood from the paulownia tree and banded with copper strips. *Han giri* are expensive, but they are readily available in Japanese hardware stores or large Asian markets. You can also use any large wooden bowl that isn't oily and doesn't smell like salad dressing. If you don't have a wooden bowl that is pristine, a medium-large plastic, metal, or glass bowl works fine.

You will also need something to blow cool air on the rice while you mix it. A hand fan or a folded-up newspaper is okay in a pinch, but many Japanese home cooks just aim an electric fan at the bowl. One friend uses a hair dryer set on "cool." That delivers a nicely focused stream of air and is especially good if you have a friend there to hold it steady. (A blow dryer or a hand fan is tricky to juggle by yourself.)

1. Wash the rice thoroughly. Place the rice in the rice cooker bowl and fill the bowl about half-full with cold tap water. Swirl the rice in the water with your hand. Carefully pour off most of the water, holding one cupped hand under the stream to catch any grains of rice carried away with the water. Holding the bowl steady with one hand, use the other to rub and squeeze the wet rice, turning the bowl as you go so that all the rice is "scrubbed." (One friend calls this giving the rice a massage, and you definitely do want to use some muscle power.) The small amount of water in the bowl will turn chalky white. Now, run cold water into the bowl, give the rice a quick swish, and carefully drain off the water as before. Repeat the scrubbing and pouring-off process twice more. By the third time, the water you pour off will be nearly clear.

2. Add the cooking water. Some cooks like to use bottled water; do this if you are not crazy about the taste of your tap water. (Note that you are using slightly less water than the regular 3-cup (700 ml) level marker on your cooker bowl; the exact amount depends on how much water remains in your washed and drained rice.) Let the rice soak in the rice cooker bowl for 30 minutes if your machine has a built-in soak period, 45 minutes if it doesn't.

3. Add the sake to the rice. Close the cover and set for the Regular or Sushi cycle.

4. While the rice is cooking, prepare the vinegar mixture. In a small saucepan, combine the vinegar, sugar, and salt. Simmer over medium heat, stirring occasionally, just until the salt and sugar melt. Or you can heat the vinegar mixture in a microwave oven. Remove from the heat and allow to cool to room temperature.

5. While the rice is cooking, lay out the following items around your workspace. When the rice is done, you will have to act quickly, so everything should be assembled and available within arm's reach.

- a clean dishcloth or cloth napkin, rinsed in cool water and wrung out
- a *han giri*, a clean bowl, wooden (if it is pristine), plastic, metal, or glass (if your bowl is wooden, rinse it out with cool water to prevent the rice from sticking)

2¼ cups (450 g) or (3 rice cooker cups) high-quality Japanese-style short- or medium-grain rice
About 2¼ cups (535 ml) water
2 tablespoons (60 ml) sake
¼ cup (28 ml) unseasoned rice vinegar
1½ to 2 tablespoons (20 to 26 g) sugar, to your taste
1 teaspoon salt

(Continued on next page)

Sushi Rice, *continued*

- the plastic rice spatula that came with your cooker, rinsed in cool water
- your vinegar mixture, at room temperature
- an electric fan, a hair dryer with a "cool" setting, a hand fan, or a folded newspaper

6. When the machine switches to the Keep Warm cycle, let the rice steam for 15 minutes. Then, use the spatula to scoop all the rice into the bowl. Holding the spatula in one hand (with the curved back side facing up) over the rice and the pan with the vinegar mixture in the other, slowly pour the vinegar over the spatula, letting it run off and fall lightly onto the rice. Move the spatula around the bowl as you pour. The net effect will be to sprinkle the vinegar as evenly as possible over the surface of the rice. Gently nestle the damp cloth over the rice, covering it completely and bunching up the cloth against the sides of the bowl. Wait 2 minutes.

7. Mix and cool the rice. You want rice that is shiny, body temperature or a bit cooler, mostly dry, and fairly sticky. The grains should be distinct, not mashed. Force-cooling the rice keeps it from absorbing the vinegar and getting too sticky.

8. Aim the electric fan at the rice in the bowl (or get your hair dryer or hand fan ready), but don't turn it on yet. Mix the rice with the spatula, holding the spatula vertically and using it like a knife, gently and repeatedly cutting through and lifting sections of rice. (If you stirred the rice in the traditional manner, you would quickly make rice mush.) Rotate the bowl so that all of the rice gets mixed. After 1 minute of mixing, turn the fan to low or medium speed (or begin to use the hair dryer or to fan the rice by hand). Continue "cutting," lifting, fanning, and turning the bowl until the rice is shiny and about body temperature (feel it with your palm). The rice is now ready to use.

9. If you are not ready to assemble your sushi, just set the spatula on top of the rice and re-cover the rice with the towel. The rice can wait, covered with the towel, for about an hour or so.

Maki Sushi

▶ YIELD: 6 rolls; serves 4 to 8

Maki are seaweed-wrapped rolls of rice with something tasty centered inside. The rolls are sliced to expose a cross section of the fillings, which range from the extremely simple, like cucumber strips, to the inventive, like California rolls, the crab, avocado, sesame, and cucumber combination that indeed was created in the United States. *Maki* sushi is typically made in three thicknesses; medium (about 1½ inches (3.8 cm) across) is the easiest to handle. You can be as creative as you want, but remember that anything used to stuff *maki* sushi should be soft. Raw cucumber is okay, but carrot strips should be cooked.

The only piece of special equipment you will need is a *maki-su*, the little bamboo-and-string mat used to support the seaweed while you roll it around the rice and fillings (it looks like a miniature window shade). These cost only a few dollars and are easy to find in Asian markets, import stores like Cost Plus, cookware shops, or health food stores. (Or substitute a piece of heavy-duty aluminum foil.) The dried seaweed wrappers, *yaki sushi nori*, wasabi, and ginger are all sold in Asian markets, health food stores, and gourmet markets.

Here we provide general directions for making *maki* sushi, followed by a selection of common, easy-to-prepare fillings.

1. Arrange around your work surface for assembly:

- the sushi rice in its cloth-covered bowl
- the sheets of *nori*
- your fillings
- a bamboo rolling mat for forming the rolls, or a 9 × 10-inch (23 × 25 cm) sheet of heavy-duty aluminum foil
- 2 forks
- a clean, damp dishcloth
- a sharp chef's knife
- a plastic or wooden cutting board
- a small saucer of rice vinegar (may be needed to seal the rolls)
- a serving platter (a cake plate or small square platter works nicely)
- condiments in serving bowls

1 recipe Sushi Rice (page 94)

6 sheets of *yaki sushi nori* (toasted seaweed sheets)

Desired fillings (see page 99)

Soy sauce, ready-to-eat wasabi (sold in a plastic tube or as a powder that you mix with water to make the paste), and slices of pickled ginger, for serving

(Continued on next page)

2. Arrange the rolling mat in front of you, with the pieces of bamboo running horizontally (parallel to the edge of the work surface). Place a piece of *nori* on the mat, with the smoother side down.

3. Uncover the rice and use the spatula to section the rice into 6 parts. Scoop out one section and place it on the bottom half of the sheet of *nori*. Re-cover the remaining rice to keep it from drying out. Hold a fork in each hand, tines down, rounded side up. Use the forks like garden rakes to spread out the rice as evenly as possible over the bottom two-thirds of the *nori*. Don't leave any margins; spread the rice all the way to the edges. About 1 inch (2.5 cm) up from the bottom, use the side of a fork to push aside some of the rice and make a sort of depression or trough where the filling will go. The trough should extend all the way across the *nori*. Don't expose the *nori*, though; you want your filling to be enclosed in a layer of rice.

4. Lay the desired filling in the trough. It is okay to mound it rather high. You will compress it as you complete the roll. (You will quickly learn how much filling to use to produce a roll that is neither skimpy nor bulging.)

5. Slide the *nori* to the edge of the mat closest to you. Lifting the mat, not the *nori*, begin the roll by bringing the strip of rice closest to you to meet the strip of rice on the other side of the filling. Squeeze the mat gently but firmly, moving your hands along the entire length of the mat, to create a nice, even log shape. Now complete the roll, stopping every so often to gently squeeze the mat and shape the roll. At the end, give a final squeeze, hard enough to firm and seal the roll but not so hard that the filling oozes out the ends. If the *nori* doesn't seal, dip your finger in vinegar and wet the edge of the *nori*.

6. Set the finished roll aside and continue filling and rolling the remaining 5 sheets of *nori*.

7. When all the rolls are finished, cut each into 6 pieces. You will make the cleanest cuts if you use a wet knife, wipe it with the damp towel after every cut, and cut with a back-and-forth sawing motion instead of pressing down. Arrange the rolls cut side up on the serving platter. Serve with the soy sauce, wasabi, and pickled ginger.

SOME FILLINGS FOR MAKI SUSHI

- **CUCUMBER: Japanese cucumbers are small, slender, and less watery than the American or even the long English ones.** If you can't find Japanese cucumbers, the English variety is a good substitute. To cut them for sushi: Cut the unpeeled cucumber on the diagonal into slices about ¼ inch (6 mm) thick, forming long ovals. Stack the ovals and cut into thin matchsticks. If you use English cucumbers, you may want to let the pieces wait for you on a double layer of paper towels so that any extra moisture is absorbed.

- **RADISH SPROUTS: These long white sprouts topped by delicate green leaves make a tasty, slightly spicy addition to sushi rolls.** To use, trim away the roots, then wash the sprouts by swishing them gently in a bowl of cold water. Let dry on a double layer of paper towels.

- **SHIITAKE MUSHROOMS: Dried shiitake mushrooms are softened by soaking in water, then seasoned by simmering in a small amount of flavorful liquid.** They are a very tasty and popular sushi filling. To prepare 8 medium-size dried shiitake mushrooms: Place the mushrooms in a small bowl; add water to just cover. Let the mushrooms soak until softened, 2 to 4 hours at room temperature. (If you are short on time, soak in hot water for 1 hour, or cover the bowl of mushrooms and water tightly with plastic wrap and microwave for 2 minutes on HIGH power. Allow to cool before proceeding.) Squeeze any liquid from the mushrooms, reserving it. Cut the tough stems from the mushrooms and slice the mushrooms into matchsticks. Slowly pour the mushroom soaking liquid into a small saucepan, being careful to leave any grit behind in the bowl. To the saucepan add about 2 tablespoons (28 ml) each sake, mirin (sweet rice wine), and soy sauce. Add ¼ teaspoon salt and, if desired, ½ teaspoon chicken bouillon granules (or ½ cube). Add the mushrooms and cook over medium-high heat until most of the liquid is absorbed. Remove the mushrooms from any remaining liquid.

  If you want to use fresh shiitakes for sushi, skip the soaking step and season by cooking them with sake, mirin, and soy sauce as above, adding a bit of Vegetarian Dashi (page 105), if needed.

- **SCRAMBLED EGGS: Finely crumbled, seasoned scrambled eggs are popular as a rice topping as well as a sushi filling.** They are a lot easier to make than the thin Japanese omelets. Beat 2 eggs in a bowl with ½ teaspoon potato starch (also called potato starch flour; do not use regular potato flour! If you don't have an Asian market in your town, you can find potato starch with the kosher foods in large supermarkets), ½ teaspoon water, 2 rounded teaspoons sugar, ½ teaspoon salt, and 2 drops soy sauce. Coat an 8-inch (20 cm) skillet with nonstick cooking spray. Place the skillet over high heat. When it is hot, add the egg mixture and cook, stirring with chopsticks or a spatula to break up the egg into firm but tender fine crumbles. Let cool before using.

- **RAW TUNA: If you can buy sushi-quality tuna in your town, by all means go ahead! It makes simple and delicious** *maki*. Just cut the tuna into strips the thickness of a pencil. You can add radish sprouts if desired. One-half pound (225 g) of tuna will fill 6 rolls very generously.

California Rolls

▶ YIELD: 3 rolls; serves 2 to 4

These rolls are made with cooked crabmeat, but shrimp-filled California rolls are the stars of the sushi platter at a Japanese restaurant in the shrimp-fishing town of Mazatlán, Mexico. Substitute ¼ pound (115 g) poached shrimp, shelled and finely chopped, for the crabmeat.

1. Using two forks or your fingers, finely shred the crabmeat. Mix the crabmeat with a dab of Chinese mustard and enough mayonnaise to hold the crab together; start with 1 or 2 teaspoons. Add more mustard if you want a spicier flavor.

2. To prepare the avocado, cut it in half the long way, working your knife around the pit. Remove the pit and use a knife to score the avocado into slices about ⅓ inch (8 mm) thick. Don't cut all the way through the skin. Use a large soup spoon to scoop the slices right out of the avocado shell. If the avocado is large, you may wish to halve the slices lengthwise. Prepare the cucumbers as described on page 99.

3. For each California *maki*, spread the rice on the *nori* as described on page 98. In the trough, layer the crab salad, cucumber, and avocado strips. Sprinkle the rice generously with the sesame seeds. Roll up carefully and cut each *maki* into 6 pieces, wiping the knife with a damp towel between cuts.

4. Serve with soy sauce and wasabi paste for dipping.

5. *Note:* Toasted Japanese sesame seeds are light tan and sold in a shaker jar in Japanese markets; they are larger and more flavorful than ordinary sesame seeds and have already been toasted; toast them again in a small skillet to enhance the flavor.

¼ pound (115 g) cooked crabmeat, picked over for shells and cartilage

1 to 4 teaspoons (5 to 20 g) Chinese (hot) mustard, to your taste

1 to 4 teaspoons (5 to 20 g) mayonnaise, to your taste

1 medium-size avocado (Hass is best.)

1 to 2 Japanese cucumbers or part of a long English one

½ recipe Sushi Rice (page 94)

3 sheets *yaki sushi nori* (toasted seaweed sheets)

Toasted Japanese sesame seeds (see Note)

Soy sauce and wasabi paste, for serving

Chirashi Sushi (Osaka Style)

▸ MACHINE: Medium (6-cup [1.4 L]) or large (10-cup) rice cooker; fuzzy logic or on/off
▸ CYCLE: Regular or Sushi ▸ YIELD: Serves 10 to 12

4⅛ cups (825 g) or
   5½ rice cooker cups
   high-quality sushi rice
About 4⅛ cups (975 ml)
   water
¾ cup (175 ml) rice vinegar
¾ cup (150 g) sugar
1 teaspoon salt

INGREDIENT LAYERS
Kampyo (dried gourd strips;
   page 104)
Grated Carrots (page 104)
Seasoned Shiitake Mush-
   rooms (page 105)
Peas (page 105) or snow
   peas
Japanese Omelet (page
   104)
1 teaspoon to 4 table-
   spoons red pickled ginger
   strips (*beni shoga*), to
   your taste
About ¼ ounce *kizami*
   (shredded) *nori* (about 1
   loosely packed cup)

In Tokyo, *chirashi* sushi is like unconstructed *nigiri* or *maki* sushi, except the ingredients are layered in a bowl. It is typically made with slices of raw fish, vegetables, and other ingredients, beautifully arranged on a bed of rice. In Osaka, though, *chirashi* sushi is a more casual dish, somewhat akin to a rice salad. Sometimes called *barazushi* or *maze gohan* (mixed rice), it is frequently made at home or for parties with friends and family. Like a potato salad, it is subject to the cook's skill, tastes, and whims, and the ingredients can vary enormously. Here is the way Julie's colleague Sharon Noguchi makes it. Sharon is a terrific cook whose family came to San Francisco from the Osaka area about a hundred years ago. Sharon notes that it's considered lucky to make *chirashi* sushi with an odd number of ingredients: five or seven, usually. She uses seven.

The vinegar dressing Sharon uses is much sweeter and more abundant than that used in the *maki* sushi recipe on page 97, which we learned from a Tokyo-born cook. Sharon's seasoned shiitake mushrooms, too, are sweeter and much less salty. If you like the Osaka-style sushi rice, by all means use these vinegar dressing proportions to make rice for *maki* sushi or hand rolls.

1. Make the rice: Wash it as directed for Sushi Rice (page 94). Place the rice in the rice cooker bowl. If your machine has a Sushi cycle, add the amount of water directed. If not, add the water so that it's under the 5-cup (1.2 L) water line in the rice cooker bowl. Soak the rice for about 30 minutes. Set for the Regular or Sushi cycle.

2. In a small saucepan, combine the vinegar, sugar, and salt and heat on the stove or in a microwave oven just until the sugar and salt melt. Let the mixture cool. (If you're short on time, cool it quickly by placing the container in a larger bowl of ice water.)

3. When the rice is ready, prepare it as described in steps 6 and 7 for Sushi Rice. Cover it with a clean, damp towel and leave at room temperature until you are ready to proceed.

4. Uncover your prepared rice and add the prepared *kampyo*, carrots, and mushrooms. Mix well with a dampened rice spatula, holding the spatula vertically and using the same cutting and lifting motions you did to mix the rice and vinegar.

5. Arrange the rice in a large serving bowl. Smooth the top without smashing the rice. Top the rice with the peas in a single layer, then with the omelet strips. Arrange a few red pickled ginger strips decoratively on top of the omelet strips or just make a little pile in the center.

6. Just before serving (you don't want it to get soggy), sprinkle on the *nori* strips. If you can't find *kizami nori*, buy *ajitsuke* (seasoned) *nori* in strips and use scissors to cut the strips into fine shreds.

7. *Chirashi* sushi can be made several hours ahead of time. If you are making *chirashi* sushi 2 hours or less before you intend to serve it, complete the dish up through the ginger topping and let it rest, tightly covered, at cool room temperature. Add the *nori* just before serving.

8. If you must make *chirashi* sushi 2 to about 8 hours ahead, complete the recipe up through adding the peas. Store the *chirashi* sushi tightly covered at room temperature. An oversize plastic container with a snap-on lid is perfect for this—authentic Tupperware will preserve it best. Refrigerate the omelet strips, tightly covered. When you are ready to serve, finish assembling the dish, adding the *nori* at the very last minute.

Kampyo (Dried Gourd Strips)

About 1 ounce (28 g) kampyo
4 teaspoons (24 g) salt
1 cup (235 ml) plus 2 tablespoons (28 ml) water
2 tablespoons sugar
2 to 3 tablespoons (28 to 45 ml) soy sauce, to your taste
¼ cup Vegetarian (60 ml) Dashi (page 105)
1 tablespoon (75 ml) sake

1. Place the kampyo in a bowl with the salt and 2 tablespoons (28 ml) of the water. Knead it with your hands for a few minutes, rubbing the salt into the strips. Add the remaining 1 cup (235 ml) of water and let soak for 20 minutes.

2. Massage the softened kampyo strips with your fingers, smoothing out any that are curled up. Drain the salted water from the bowl, add fresh cool water to the bowl, and massage the kampyo underwater to remove as much salt as possible. Drain and rinse again.

3. Place the kampyo in a small saucepan with the sugar, soy sauce, vegetarian dashi, and sake. Bring to a boil and then reduce the heat to a simmer. Cover the kampyo (not the pan) with a circle of parchment paper cut just a bit smaller than the diameter of the pan, a small saucer, the lid to a slightly smaller pan, or an *otoshi buta*, a flat wooden drop lid designed to keep simmering items submerged and yet allow some steam to escape. (They are sold in several sizes in Japanese markets or hardware stores.) Let the kampyo cook about 15 minutes, stirring occasionally, until most of the liquid is absorbed. The kampyo will be shiny and amber-colored. It should be tender, not rubbery; if it's not tender, cook it longer. Drain.

4. When the kampyo is cool enough to work with, line up the strands on a cutting board and dice.

Japanese Omelet

2 large or extra-large eggs
1 teaspoon sugar
1 tablespoon (15 ml) mirin (sweet rice wine) or sake (for a less sweet omelet)
Pinch of salt
1 teaspoon mild vegetable oil

1. Lightly beat the eggs in a small bowl with the sugar, mirin, and salt.

2. Coat a 10-inch (25.4 cm) nonstick skillet with the vegetable oil. Heat the skillet over low heat. Pour in the egg mixture, cover the skillet, and cook, undisturbed, until the egg is set but not browned, about 2 minutes or longer, if needed.

3. Flip the omelet out of the pan and onto a cutting board. (If the omelet is cooked through, it should pop right out.) A perfect omelet will be all yellow, with no browned spots.

4. When the omelet is cool enough to handle, cut into 2-inch (5 cm) -wide strips. Stack the strips and slice into thin slivers.

Grated Carrots

1 large or 2 medium-size carrots
1½ cups (355 ml) Vegetarian Dashi (page 105)
¼ teaspoon salt

1. Peel and grate the carrots.

2. Bring the vegetarian dashi and salt to a boil in a small saucepan. Add the carrots. When the liquid returns to a boil, immediately drain the carrots and run cold water over them to stop the cooking.

Seasoned Shiitake Mushrooms

6 large dried shiitake mushrooms
½ cup (120 ml) Vegetarian Dashi (below)
⅓ cup (80 ml) soy sauce
¼ cup (50 g) sugar
3 tablespoons (45 ml) sake

1. Place the mushrooms in a small bowl; add warm water to just cover. Let the mushrooms soak until softened, 2 to 4 hours at room temperature. (If you are short on time, soak in hot water for 1 hour or cover the bowl of mushrooms and water tightly with plastic wrap and microwave for 2 minutes on HIGH power. Allow to cool before proceeding.)

2. Drain and cut the mushrooms into ⅛-inch (3 mm)-wide strips or as thinly as possible, discarding the stems.

3. Combine the vegetarian dashi, soy sauce, sugar, and sake in a small saucepan over medium-high heat. When the mixture boils, add the mushroom slices and stir. Reduce the heat to a simmer. Cover the mushrooms (not the pan) with a circle of parchment paper cut just a bit smaller than the diameter of the pan, a small saucer, the lid to a slightly smaller pan, or an *otoshi buta*, a flat wooden drop lid designed to keep simmering items submerged and yet allow some steam to escape. (They are sold in several sizes in Japanese markets or hardware stores.) Let the mushrooms simmer slowly for about 20 minutes. Most of the liquid will be absorbed or evaporated and the mushrooms will have turned a caramel color. Drain any remaining liquid.

Peas

1½ cups (355 ml) Vegetarian Dashi (page 105)
1 teaspoon salt
1 package (12 ounces, or 340 g) of frozen petite peas

1. Bring the vegetarian dashi and salt to a boil in a medium-size saucepan. Add the peas and cook briefly, about 1 minute, just until thawed and separate. Drain the peas and cool quickly under cold running water.

2. Snow Peas: Substitute 2 cups (126 g) of snow peas, trimmed of tough strings and sliced on the diagonal into ¼-inch (6 mm)-wide strips.

Vegetarian Dashi

1 5-inch (13 cm) strip of dried kombu seaweed
1¾ cups (410 ml) water
1½ tablespoons (25 ml) low-sodium soy sauce
1 tablespoon (15 ml) sake
1 tablespoon (15 ml) mirin

Place the water and kombu in a medium saucepan. Let soak at least 30 minutes on the counter or overnight in the refrigerator. Bring to a simmer over medium-high heat. When the water just begins to bubble and boil, add the soy sauce, sake, and mirin. Remove from the heat and immediately remove the kombu. Let cool to lukewarm and use immediately or store in the refrigerator overnight. Reserve the seaweed for another dish.

WHOLE-GRAIN COOKING

Basic Pearled Barley — 107

Zucchini Couscous — 107

Israeli Couscous with Orange — 108

Farro with Shiitakes — 109

Basic Buckwheat Groats — 110

Five-Grain Pilaf — 111

Millet, Winter Squash, and Sweet Pea Pilaf — 112

Quinoa Mushroom Pilaf — 114

Curry, Quinoa, Lentil, and Brown Rice Pilaf — 115

Bulgur and Cherry Pilaf — 117

Wild Rice with Fennel and Dried Cranberries — 118

Just as you cook rice in your rice cooker, you can cook whole grains. You use exactly the same technique, which is to press the Regular cycle button. The machine does the rest. Be prepared for different aromas and very different textures; each whole grain has a character unto itself. Terms such as "groat" and "berry" are references to the hulled whole grain. If the bran layer on the grain is especially tough, a soak may be in order to help with the cooking. If you end up with whole grains that are too wet, just drain off the excess water as if you were cooking on the stovetop. If your grains are too dry, drizzle them with another ¼ cup (60 ml) of water and continue cooking or leave on the Keep Warm cycle. As with rice, if you turn off the machine and leave the lid closed, the inherent warmth of the environment will keep your grains warm for an hour.

Basic Pearled Barley

▶ MACHINE: Medium (6-cup [1.4 L]) rice cooker; fuzzy logic or on/off ▶ CYCLE: Brown Rice or Regular ▶ YIELD: About 3 cups; serves 4

While most of the barley grown in this country goes to brewing beer, you can still find pearled barley on most supermarket shelves. It is called pearled barley since, when cooked, it looks just like little pearl seeds. A favorite in soups because of its comforting digestive quality, pearled barley is a nice alternative to rice, works well in a grain and rice combination, and can be cooked like risotto. Barley is also great in salads or stuffed peppers. Pearled barley is hulled, so it is very white, needs no soaking, and cooks in under an hour. It is not the same as what is sold as "quick barley," which is precooked and dried, and cooks up very mushy. You want barley to be chewy.

1 cup (200 g) pearled barley
2 cups (475 ml) plus 2 tablespoons (28 ml) water
Pinch of salt

1. Place the barley in the rice cooker bowl. Add the water and salt; swirl to combine. Close the cover and set for the Brown Rice or Regular cycle.

2. When the machine switches to the Keep Warm cycle, let the barley steam for 15 minutes. If there is water left over, drain it off; if it is too dry, drizzle with hot water, 1 tablespoon at a time, and let steam until the barley has the right texture. Fluff with a wooden or plastic rice paddle or wooden spoon, and let the barley cool in the bowl or serve hot. It will hold on Keep Warm for up to 1 hour.

Zucchini Couscous

▶ MACHINE: Medium (6-cup [1.4 L]) rice cooker; fuzzy logic or on/off ▶ CYCLE: Quick Cook and/or Regular ▶ YIELD: Serves 4

With zucchini and chickpeas, this is a quick and filling couscous to whip up for dinner. Chickpeas have a natural affinity for couscous; wait until you taste them together.

2 tablespoons (28 ml) olive oil
1½ pounds (680 g) zucchini, cut into ½-inch (1.3 cm) cubes
½ teapoon ground cumin
1 cup (235 ml) water
1 cup (175 g) couscous, refined or whole wheat
1 cup (240 g) canned chickpeas, drained and rinsed

1. Set the machine for the Quick Cook or Regular cycle. Place the oil in the rice cooker bowl. When hot, add the zucchini and cumin. Cook, stirring a few times, just to take the raw edge off of the cumin, about 2 minutes. Add the water, couscous, and chickpeas; swirl to combine. Close the cover and reset for the Regular cycle or let the Regular cycle complete.

2. When the machine switches to the Keep Warm cycle, let the couscous steam for 5 minutes. Fluff with a wooden or plastic rice paddle or wooden spoon. This couscous will hold on Keep Warm for up to 1 hour. Serve hot.

Israeli Couscous with Orange

▶ MACHINE: Medium (6-cup [1.4 L]) rice cooker; fuzzy logic or on/off ▶ CYCLE: Quick Cook and/or Regular
▶ YIELD: Serves 4

1 tablespoon (15 ml) extra-virgin olive oil

1 medium-size shallot, minced

1 cup (171 g) Israeli couscous

2 cups (475 ml) chicken stock

½ teaspoon salt, if unsalted stock is used

½ teaspoon grated orange zest

2 tablespoons (18 g) finely chopped fresh Italian parsley leaves

Israeli couscous is larger than regular couscous, and the little pasta bits are perfectly round. It is a type of couscous growing in popularity in the United States and no wonder. It is tender, with a slightly toasty taste, and it takes happily to almost any kind of herb or seasoning. It cooks up beautifully in the rice cooker. The brand we found is Osem, which is imported from Israel. This savory dish is positively addicting.

1. Set the rice cooker for the Quick Cook or Regular cycle. Place the olive oil in the rice cooker bowl. When hot, add the shallot and let soften in the oil, 1 to 2 minutes. Stir in the couscous and cook until aromatic and lightly browned, 2 to 3 minutes. Add the chicken stock and salt, if needed. Close the cover and reset for the Regular cycle or let the Regular cycle complete.

2. When the machine switches to the Keep Warm cycle, let the couscous steam for 10 minutes. Open the cover and add the orange zest and parsley. Fluff with a wooden or plastic rice paddle or wooden spoon to loosen the grains and blend in the orange zest and parsley. This couscous will hold on Keep Warm for up to 1 hour. Serve hot or warm.

VARIATIONS:

Israeli Couscous with Orange and Olives: Omit the parsley. Stir in 2 tablespoons (18 g) of sliced pitted Kalamata olives with the orange zest.

Israeli Couscous with Orange and Almonds: Omit the parsley. Stir in 2 tablespoons (14 g) of toasted slivered almonds with the orange zest.

Israeli Couscous with Mushrooms: Omit the orange zest. Increase the olive oil to 2 tablespoons (28 ml). Sauté ½ cup (35 g) sliced fresh mushrooms along with the shallot.

Farro with Shiitakes

▸ MACHINE: Medium (6-cup [1.4 L]) rice cooker; fuzzy logic or on/off ▸ CYCLE: Quick Cook and/or Regular
▸ YIELD: Serves 3 to 4

The rich, meaty flavor and texture of fresh shiitake mushrooms is a great foil to the chewy whole-grain Italian spelt. Serve with roast chicken or beef dishes.

1. Set the rice cooker for the Quick Cook or Regular cycle. Place the butter in the rice cooker bowl. When melted, add the shallots and stir to coat with the butter. Add the mushrooms and close the cover. Let the shallots and mushrooms cook, stirring occasionally, until completely soft, about 7 minutes.

2. Open the cover, add the farro, and stir to combine. Continue to cook, stirring occasionally, until the farro smells toasty, about 3 minutes. Add the water, salt, pepper to taste, and herb sprig. Close the cover and reset for the Regular cycle or let the Regular cycle complete.

3. When the machine switches to the Keep Warm cycle, remove the herb sprig and let the farro steam for 10 minutes. Fluff with a wooden or plastic rice paddle or wooden spoon. This farro will hold on Keep Warm for 1 hour. Serve hot.

2 tablespoons (28 g) unsalted butter
1 large or 2 small shallots, finely chopped
6 ounces (170 g) fresh shiitake mushrooms, stems removed and caps chopped (2 medium-large)
1 cup (208 g) farro
1½ cups (355 ml) water
Pinch of salt
Freshly ground black pepper
Small sprig of fresh savory, marjoram, or oregano

Basic Buckwheat Groats

▶ MACHINE: Medium (6-cup [1.4 L]) rice cooker; fuzzy logic or on/off ▶ CYCLE: Brown Rice or Regular
▶ YIELD: About 2½ cups; serves 3 to 4

1 cup (164 g) unroasted white buckwheat groats
2 cups (475 ml) water or chicken stock
1 tablespoon (14 g) unsalted butter or (15 g) walnut oil
Pinch of salt, if unsalted sunflower seeds are used
½ cup (73 g) shelled sunflower seeds or (50 g) walnuts, toasted

Unroasted buckwheat groats, also called white buckwheat, have a much milder flavor than roasted groats. You can immediately tell them apart—the toasted groats (also known as kasha) are russet colored. Kasha is a very old and traditional cereal grain in the Russian hinterlands; the word *kasha* can also mean "meal." The Russians feel about kasha the way the Japanese feel about rice. While normally coated with egg to keep the grains separate, this version is from natural foods writer Rebecca Wood and has no egg. Buckwheat is an acquired taste to the uninitiated. Use fresh groats; we mail-order them from Birkett Mills in New York. If you use the delicious Japanese heirloom miniature buckwheat called *soba gome,* follow this recipe but reduce the liquid by ½ cup (120 ml) and omit the sunflower seeds or nuts.

1. Place the groats in a dry skillet over medium-high heat. Toast, stirring constantly, until the color deepens a few shades, about 4 minutes. You can toast groats light or dark, to your own preference.

2. Place the groats in the rice cooker bowl. Add the water, butter, salt, if using, and sunflower seeds; swirl to combine. Close the cover and set for the Brown Rice or Regular cycle.

3. When the machine switches to the Keep Warm cycle, let the groats steam for 15 minutes. Fluff the grains with a wooden or plastic rice paddle or wooden spoon. These groats will hold on Keep Warm for up to 1 hour. Serve hot.

Five-Grain Pilaf

▶ MACHINE: Medium (6-cup [1.4 L]) or large (10-cup) rice cooker; fuzzy logic or on/off
▶ CYCLE: Brown Rice or Regular ▶ YIELD: Serves 6 to 8

Grain mixtures have become very popular, especially with vegans. Vegetarian restaurants often have a special daily side dish of mixed grains to serve with butter and soy sauce or to soak up juice from a stir-fry or vegetable stew. In this combination we use the Himalayan red rice since it is ever so slightly more elongated than the Bhutanese, so it is a good mixture with the long-grain brown rice. You can cool, then freeze this dish in 1- or 2-cup (235 to 475 ml) containers to be reheated in the microwave on a night when you just can't cook.

½ cup (90 g) Thai brown jasmine rice
½ cup (90 g) Himalayan red rice or Thai ruby red jasmine rice
½ cup (110 g) millet
3 tablespoons (43 g) quinoa
2 tablespoons (26 g) amaranth
2¾ cups (650 ml) water
1 teaspoon sea salt (optional)

1. Place the rices in a bowl and fill with cold water. Swish it around with your fingers. Carefully pour off the water and wash a few more times until the water is clear. Rinse and drain the millet and quinoa once in a fine mesh strainer.

2. Place all the grains in the rice cooker bowl. Add the water and salt, if using; swirl just to combine. Close the cover and set for the Brown Rice or Regular cycle.

3. When the machine switches to the Keep Warm cycle, let the grains steam for 20 minutes. Fluff the grains with a wooden or plastic rice paddle or wooden spoon. This dish will hold for 2 hours on Keep Warm. Serve hot.

Millet, Winter Squash, and Sweet Pea Pilaf

▶ MACHINE: Medium (6-cup [1.4 L]) rice cooker; fuzzy logic or on/off ▶ CYCLE: Regular ▶ YIELD: Serves 4

1 cup (220 g) millet, rinsed and drained in a mesh strainer

1 small white or red boiling onion, diced (about 3 tablespoons [30 g])

2 cups (280 g) peeled and cubed (¾-inch [1.9 cm]) winter squash (The ready-cut 8-ounce [225 g] package of cubed butternut squash in the produce section is the right amount.)

¾ cup (98 g) thawed frozen petite peas or (113 g) shelled fresh peas

2 cups (475 ml) water

¼ teaspoon turmeric

Pinch of sea salt

Cubed winter squash and frozen peas are an easy combination with millet for a different kind of weeknight side dish. Millet is gluten free and should be stored in a tightly closed container, preferably glass, in a cool, dry place or in the refrigerator, where it will keep for up to two years.

1. Place the millet, onion, squash, and peas in the rice cooker bowl. Add the water, turmeric, and salt; swirl just to combine. Close the cover and set for the Regular cycle.

2. When the machine switches to the Keep Warm cycle, let the millet steam for at least 10 minutes. Gently fluff the millet with a wooden or plastic rice paddle or wooden spoon. This pilaf will hold for 1 hour on Keep Warm. Serve hot.

Quinoa Mushroom Pilaf

▶ MACHINE: Medium (6-cup [1.4 L]) rice cooker; fuzzy logic or on/off ▶ CYCLE: Quick Cook and/or Regular
▶ YIELD: Serves 3 to 4

1 tablespoon (15 ml)
   olive oil
1 tablespoon (14 g) butter
¾ cup (120 g) chopped
   onion
1 clove of garlic, minced
1½ cups (105 g) sliced
   fresh mushrooms of your
   choice (all one type or a
   mixture)
1 cup (173 g) ivory quinoa,
   rinsed in cold water in a
   fine-mesh strainer until
   the water runs clear
1½ cups (355 ml) chicken
   broth
1 teaspoon chopped fresh
   thyme
1 teaspoon mushroom
   powder (optional; see
   headnote)
½ teaspoon salt, if using
   unsalted broth

The savory mushroom flavor in this pilaf gets an extra push from the mushroom powder, which is simply dried mushrooms ground to a powder. Julie discovered this amazingly versatile flavor booster when she received some as a gift. It's hard to find in stores but easy to make your own. Just break dried mushrooms into pieces a half-inch (1.3 cm) or so on a side, then grind to a fine powder in a blender (not a food processor, which can't grind them finely enough). A blend that includes the strongly flavored shiitake is nice, or create your own blend. Mushroom powder will keep for months in tightly closed glass jar.

1. Set the rice cooker for the Quick Cook or Regular cycle. Place the olive oil and butter in the rice cooker bowl. When the butter is melted, add the onion, garlic, and mushrooms. Cook, stirring a few times, until softened, about 10 minutes. Add the quinoa, broth, thyme, and mushroom powder and salt, if using; stir just to combine. Close the cover and reset for the Regular cycle or let the Regular cycle complete.

2. When the machine switches to the Keep Warm cycle, let the quinoa steam for 10 minutes. Fluff the quinoa with a wooden or plastic rice paddle or wooden spoon. This pilaf will hold on Keep Warm for 2 to 3 hours. Serve hot.

Curry, Quinoa, Lentil, and Brown Rice Pilaf

▶ MACHINE: Medium (6-cup [1.4 L]) rice cooker; fuzzy logic or on/off ▶ CYCLE: Regular ▶ YIELD: Serves: 4 to 5

Here's a lovely grain and legume combination flavored with curry powder. Commercial curry powder comes in two basic styles: mild or sweet and the hotter of the two, known as "Madras" curry powder. Red curry blends are a complex mix of select spices, chiles, and cardamom. You can gently toast the curry powder in a dry skillet until fragrant if you like to blossom your spices.

Look for small dried Thai chiles, if you can find them. (Other dried chiles, like those from the American Southwest, are much larger.)

⅔ cup (116 g) ivory quinoa
⅔ cup (123 g) long-grain brown rice
⅓ cup (64 g) brown or French green lentils, picked over
1 tablespoon (6 g) curry powder
1 bay leaf
1 dried red chile
3 cups (700 ml) water
1 to 2 tablespoons (15 to 28 ml) olive oil
1 teaspoon salt

1. Soak the quinoa for 15 minutes in a bowl in water to cover. If you don't have time for a longer soaking, use hot water and soak for 5 minutes. Stir the quinoa with your hand and carefully pour off the rinsing water until the suds disappear, using a fine mesh strainer.

2. Place the quinoa, rice, lentils, curry, bay leaf, and chile in the rice cooker bowl. Add the water, oil, and salt; swirl to combine. Close the cover and set for the Regular cycle.

3. When the machine switches to the Keep Warm cycle, let the grains steam for 10 minutes. Discard the bay leaf and chile. Fluff with a wooden or plastic rice paddle or wooden spoon. This pilaf will hold on Keep Warm for 2 hours. Serve hot.

Bulgur and Cherry Pilaf

▶ MACHINE: Medium (6-cup [1.4 L]) rice cooker; fuzzy logic or on/off ▶ CYCLE: Quick Cook and/or Regular
▶ YIELD: Serves 4 to 6

Turkish cooking pairs sweet and savory flavor elements, such as rice pilafs with fresh and dried fruit. We were surprised to learn that Turkish cooking is considered one of the great cuisines of the world, along with those of France and Italy, an inheritance left over from the Ottoman Empire, whose sultans placed high priority on their elaborate palace kitchens and full-time, dedicated-for-life chefs. The imperial cooks were tested and hired on the merit of their method of cooking rice, the most simple of dishes.

Here bulgur wheat, which has the most buttery rich flavor of all the grains, is cooked with fresh and dried cherries. Fennel seed is an integral part of Mediterranean cuisine; its flavor just sings in this preparation.

1. Set the rice cooker for the Quick Cook or Regular cycle. Place the butter in the rice cooker bowl. When the butter is melted, add the fennel seeds and bulgur; stir to coat and thoroughly heat the grains, 3 to 4 minutes; the bulgur should smell toasty.

2. Add the water and a few pinches of salt. Add the fresh and dried cherries. Stir just to combine, close the cover, and reset for the Regular cycle or let the Regular cycle complete.

3. When the machine switches to the Keep Warm cycle, lay a double layer of paper towels inside on top of the bulgur. Close the cover and let the pilaf steam for 15 minutes. Discard the paper towels and gently fluff the pilaf with a wooden or plastic rice paddle or wooden spoon. This dish will hold for 1 hour on Keep Warm. To serve, mound into a wide bowl or onto a small heated platter, and serve with a dollop of the yogurt or sprinkled with the feta. Serve hot.

1 tablespoon (14 g) butter
1 teaspoon fennel seeds or aniseed, ground in a mortar and pestle
1⅓ cups (229 g) medium or coarse bulgur
2¼ cups (535 ml) water
Salt
4 to 5 ounces (115 to 140 g) fresh Bing cherries, pitted and halved, or frozen pitted Bing cherries, thawed and halved
¼ cup (40 g) dried tart cherries (We like to use a cherry–golden raisin mixture.)
1 cup (230 g) plain Greek yogurt or ⅓ cup (50 g) crumbled feta cheese, for serving (optional)

Wild Rice with Fennel and Dried Cranberries

▸ MACHINE: Medium (6-cup [1.4 L]) rice cooker; fuzzy logic or on/off ▸ CYCLE: Brown Rice or Regular
▸ YIELD: Serves 4

1 cup (160 g) plus 2 table-spoons (20 g) wild rice

2 cups (475 ml) plus 2 tablespoons (28 ml) chicken stock

⅔ cup (160 ml) reduced-sugar or unsweetened cranberry juice cocktail or unsweetened cranberry juice

3 tablespoons (25 g) dried cranberries

2 tablespoons (28 g) unsalted butter

1 shallot, chopped

1 small bulb fennel, stalks and greens discarded, bulb chopped (about 1¼ cups [110 g])

Salt

Freshly ground black pepper

This recipe has the wild rice cooked in a combination of chicken stock and cranberry juice. A great addition to Thanksgiving dinner!

1. Place the rice in the rice cooker bowl. Add the stock and cranberry juice; stir a few times to combine. Close the cover and set for the Brown Rice or Regular cycle.

2. When the machine switches to the Keep Warm cycle, add the cranberries, close the cover, and let the rice steam for 15 minutes.

3. While the rice is steaming, melt the butter in a medium-size sauté pan over medium heat. Add the shallot and fennel and cook, stirring, until tender, 5 to 8 minutes. Season to taste with salt and pepper. When the rice has finished steaming, stir the fennel mixture into the rice. Adjust the seasonings again and serve hot.

POLENTA, GRITS, and HOMINY

Italian Polenta — 120

French Polenta — 121

Traditional Grits — 122

Fresh Hominy — 125

Shrimp and Grits — 125

Polenta, grits, and hominy have one thing in common: they are all products made from corn. All have the delicate sweet flavor that is distinctly "corny," but each is made quite differently.

Is there any home gardener who has not tried his or her hand at a few rows of corn? The familiar tassel coming out the top of the ear, tightly covered by the husk that protects the multiple kernels that are developing in rows on the inner cob—it is a vegetable as familiar as a child's nursery rhyme. This is known as field corn, and the pleasure of corn on the cob is an American summer ritual. When this soft, juicy corn is allowed to mature and dry on the stalk, the sugar turns to starch. This is the corn that is made into myriad corn products, including polenta, grits, and hominy.

Italian Polenta

▶ MACHINE: Medium (6-cup [1.4 L]) rice cooker; fuzzy logic (preferred) or on/off ▶ CYCLE: Porridge or Regular
▶ YIELD: Serves 4

4 cups (946 ml) water
1 cup (140 g) coarse-grain yellow polenta
½ teaspoon salt
Freshly ground black pepper
¼ cup (½ stick, or 55 g) unsalted butter, or more to taste
⅔ cup (67 g) freshly grated Parmesan cheese (optional)

Italian polenta, the darling of all teachers of Italian cuisine, is labeled *farina di grano turco* on the package, the Italian name of corn since the time of Columbus. It was often made in a traditional copper polenta pot, replete with a special wooden stirring stick, that was handed down within rural families. This is a really nice, fluffy polenta that is foolproof. It uses two full cycles of the Porridge cycle. It thickens considerably during the second cycle and even spits a few times during the cooking. You can double the recipe in a large 10-cup (2.4 L) machine. Serve with the Parmesan and a pat of garlic butter for a lovely treat, or sprinkle with grated Fontina cheese.

1. Place the water in the rice cooker bowl. Add the polenta and salt; stir for 15 seconds with a wooden spoon or wooden or plastic rice paddle. Close the cover and set for the Porridge or Regular cycle. A few times during the cooking, open the cover, stir for 15 seconds, then close the cover.

2. At the end of the Porridge cycle, reset for a second Porridge cycle; the polenta needs two full cycles to lose its raw, grainy texture. At the end of the second Porridge cycle, or when the Regular cycle completes, taste the polenta and make sure the desired consistency has been reached. Stir in the butter and cheese, if using (if you are chilling the polenta for frying or grilling, or using it under seafood, like grilled pesto prawns, the cheese is not necessary).

3. This polenta will hold on Keep Warm for up to 1 hour, if necessary. Add a bit more hot water if it gets too stiff. Stir before serving.

French Polenta

▶ MACHINE: Medium (6-cup [1.4 L]) or large (10-cup) rice cooker; fuzzy logic (preferred) or on/off
▶ CYCLE: Porridge or Regular ▶ YIELD: Serves 6

The French also make cornmeal mush, which was originally brought to their country by the armies of the king of Spain in the Middle Ages. Made in all regions of France, the most famous polenta preparation is Savoy mush, and French polenta can sport toppings and additions like roasted game, stewed prunes, cheese, a variety of meat and vegetable sauces, meat pan juices, and truffles, and sometimes is an addition to soup.

1. Place the polenta and water in the rice cooker bowl; stir for 15 seconds with a wooden spoon or wooden or plastic rice paddle. Add the stock and salt and pepper and nutmeg to taste. Close the cover and set for the Porridge or Regular cycle. About every 20 minutes, open and stir for 15 seconds, then close the cooker.

2. At the end of the Porridge cycle, reset for a second Porridge cycle; the polenta needs two full cycles to lose its raw, grainy texture. At the end of the second Porridge cycle, or when the Regular cycle completes, taste the polenta to make sure the desired consistency has been reached. This polenta will hold on Keep Warm for up to 1 hour.

3. When ready to serve, spoon onto serving plates and sprinkle with the goat cheese.

2 cups (280 g) coarse-grain yellow polenta
3 cups (700 ml) water
3 cups (700 ml) chicken stock or milk
Salt
Freshly ground black pepper
Freshly grated nutmeg
6 ounces (170 g) goat cheese, crumbled, for garnish

Traditional Grits

▸ MACHINE: Medium (6-cup [1.4 L]) rice cooker; fuzzy logic (preferred) or on/off ▸ CYCLE: Porridge or Regular ▸ YIELD: Serves 4

1 cup (140 g) coarse stone-ground grits
3 cups (700 ml) water
½ teaspoon salt
3 tablespoons (42 g) unsalted butter
Ground white pepper

If you live outside the southern part of the United States, the only grits you will find in the supermarket will be instant or quick cooking. Luckily, there are excellent mail-order sources for fresh ground grits. Fresh ground grits are speckled from the bits of grain left over from the milling, so be sure to cover them first with water and let the husks rise to the top, then drain and proceed from the beginning of the recipe. If you want to use quick-cooking grits, just cook for one cycle in the rice cooker and they will still be very good.

1. If you'd like to remove the husks, combine the grits and some cold tap water in a bowl or use the rice cooker bowl; the husks will rise to the top and can be skimmed off. Drain the grits.

2. Place the grits, water, and salt in the rice cooker bowl; stir for 15 seconds with a wooden spoon or wooden or plastic rice paddle. Close the cover and set for the Porridge or Regular cycle. A few times during the cooking, open the cover and stir for 15 seconds, then close the cover.

3. At the end of the Porridge cycle, reset for a second Porridge cycle, giving the grits two full cycles to reach the optimum consistency.

4. At the end of the second Porridge cycle, or when the Regular cycle completes, stir in the butter, season to taste with pepper, and serve hot. These grits will hold on Keep Warm for up to 2 hours.

Creamy Traditional Grits: Replace 1 cup (235 ml) of the water with 1 cup (235 ml) of whole milk and omit the white pepper. This version is good served with pure maple syrup and chopped crisp bacon.

Fresh Hominy

▶ MACHINE: Medium (6-cup [1.4 L]) or large (10-cup) rice cooker; fuzzy logic or on/off ▶ CYCLE: Regular
▶ YIELD: About 4 cups (660 g)

Fresh or partially cooked frozen whole hominy needs to be cooked before using. Fresh is usually available in the meat department of supermarkets, especially around the holidays. Do not add any salt while cooking, or the kernels will never soften properly. You can use fresh hominy instead of canned in soups and stews. If you happen to use dried hominy, you will need to double the amount of water and double the cooking time. You can double this recipe in the large-capacity rice cooker.

1 pound (455 g) fresh or frozen hominy, thawed overnight in the refrigerator

1. Place the hominy in the rice cooker bowl and cover with 2 inches (5 cm) of cold water. Close the cover and set for the Regular cycle. Cook until it is tender and the kernels burst open, but are still slightly firm to the bite, 1 hour or more.

2. Remove the bowl from the rice cooker, drain off most of the liquid by pouring through a colander, and let cool to room temperature. Store in the refrigerator, covered, for up to 2 days.

Shrimp and Grits

▶ MACHINE: Medium (6-cup [1.4 L]) or large (10-cup) rice cooker; fuzzy logic (preferred) or on/off
▶ CYCLE: Porridge or Regular   ▶ YIELD: Serves 6

Beth's Aunt Joan lives in Florence, South Carolina, the heart of grits country. Shrimp and grits is real southern coastal Atlantic country food, but can now be found served at lots of southern parties and in restaurants. Here is an authentic recipe, just the way they like it in the Carolinas, which we made with Old-Fashioned Stone-Ground Speckle Yellow Grits from Blackwell Mills (decorated with a line drawing of a smiling pig in a neckerchief holding a corncob with the saying "Pig Out") that Aunt Joan sent Beth. The original recipe calls for the grits to be cooked for three hours, so run the grits through a third Porridge cycle, if you wish, for a softer consistency.

1. Combine the grits and some cold tap water in a bowl or use the rice cooker bowl; the husks will rise to the top. Drain through a mesh strainer.

2. Place the grits, water, and salt in the rice cooker bowl; stir for 15 seconds with a wooden spoon or wooden or plastic rice paddle. Close the cover and set for the Porridge or Regular cycle. A few times during the cooking, open the cover and stir for 15 seconds, then close the cover.

3. At the end of the Porridge cycle, reset for a second Porridge cycle and cook until the grits reach the desired consistency, thick like breakfast porridge. When the right consistency is achieved or the Regular cycle ends, hold on Keep Warm until the shrimp are ready.

4. Fifteen minutes before the grits are done, melt the butter in a large sauté pan over medium-high heat. Add the olive oil, hot sauce, bay leaf, garlic, lemon juice, minced parsley, minced chives, tarragon, chervil, pepper, and Worcestershire, bring to a simmer over medium heat, and add the shrimp. Cook, stirring, until the shrimp turn bright pink on both sides, 2 to 3 minutes. Remove the bay leaf.

5. Spoon the hot grits into a large serving bowl. Immediately spoon the shrimp over the grits and drizzle with the sauce from the pan. Sprinkle with the chopped parsley and chives and serve hot.

---

2 cups (280 g) coarse stone-ground grits

6 cups (1.4 L) water

1 teaspoon salt

½ cup (1 stick, or 112 g) unsalted butter or margarine

¼ cup (60 ml) olive oil

¼ teaspoon Texas Pete or Tabasco hot sauce

1 bay leaf

1 teaspoon pressed garlic

3 tablespoons (45 ml) fresh lemon juice

1 teaspoon minced fresh Italian parsley leaves

1 teaspoon minced fresh chives

½ teaspoon dried tarragon

½ teaspoon dried chervil

½ teaspoon freshly ground black pepper

2 tablespoons (28 ml) Worcestershire sauce

1 pound (455 g) miniature shrimp (90/110 count), shelled and deveined (You can buy these already shelled; look for P&Ds.)

Chopped fresh Italian parsley leaves, for garnish

Chopped fresh chives, for garnish

HOT CEREALS

Creamy Breakfast Oatmeal — 127

Hot Apple Granola — 127

Vanilla Oatmeal Crème Brûlée with Berries — 129

Maple-Cinnamon Rice Pudding — 130

Seven-Herb Rice Porridge (Nanakusagayu) — 132

Thanksgiving Jook — 135

As with the cooking of all grains, we all have a way we like our cereal cooked: smooth and loose so it is a homogeneous mush, with milk, or a bit stiff, so that the milk is a moat and the cereal can be cut into with a spoon. Open the cover and check the consistency of the cereal; give a stir with your wooden or plastic rice paddle. If it looks too stiff, simply add another ¼ to ½ cup (60 to 120 ml) of water or milk. If it looks too loose, either set for a second Porridge cycle to continue the cooking (it won't hurt the mush one bit) or hold the cereal on the Keep Warm cycle for up to two hours before serving. Hot cereals hold perfectly on the Keep Warm cycle.

How to serve your porridge is entirely a matter of personal preference. Dried or fresh fruit can be used as a topping or an ingredient to be cooked with the cereal. If refined sweeteners such as brown sugar are not in your diet, cereals can be sweetened with pure maple syrup, date sugar, or honey. Create a moat of milk, half-and-half, rice milk, soy milk, or oat milk around your hot cereal. Whatever your choice, it's good morning to you!

Creamy Breakfast Oatmeal

▶ MACHINE: Medium (6-cup [1.4 L]) rice cooker; fuzzy logic only ▶ CYCLE: Porridge ▶ YIELD: Serves 2

Oats have a reputation for contributing to health similar to a homeopathic cure. Oats and milk are said to ward off the worst of chills, as well as making a great poultice-like mask for the face. With maple syrup and sweet dried dates, plain old oatmeal is a morning feast that raises its status above that of a humble grain. Note that this recipe calls for steel-cut oats rather than rolled oats, making an exceptionally creamy porridge.

⅔ cup (117 g) steel-cut oats
1¾ cups (410 ml) milk mixed with 1 teaspoon pure vanilla extract or 1¾ cups vanilla soy milk
1¼ teaspoons ground cinnamon
Pinch of fine sea salt
2 tablespoons (28 ml) pure maple syrup
¼ cup (45 g) chopped dates

1. Place the oats, vanilla milk, cinnamon, salt, and maple syrup in the rice cooker bowl; stir gently to combine. Sprinkle with the dates. Close the cover and set for the Porridge cycle.

2. At the end of the cycle, the cereal will be thick and will hold on Keep Warm for up to 1 hour. Spoon into bowls and serve hot.

Hot Apple Granola

▶ MACHINE: Medium (6-cup [1.4 L]) rice cooker; fuzzy logic only ▶ CYCLE: Porridge ▶ YIELD: Serves 2

This hearty grain and fruit blend cooks up into a flavorful and sustaining breakfast cereal.

1 cup (120 g) Apple Granola (below)
2½ cups (570 ml) water
Pinch of fine sea salt
Cold milk or soy milk, for serving

1. Place the granola, water, and salt in the rice cooker bowl; stir gently to combine. Close the cover and set for the Porridge cycle.

2. At the end of the cycle, the cereal will be thick and will hold on Keep Warm for 1 to 2 hours. Spoon into bowls and serve hot, with a moat of milk.

Apple Granola

▶ YIELD: About 5 cups (ten 1-cup cooked servings)

1 cup (156 g) steel-cut oats
1 cup (120 g) cracked wheat
1 cup (120 g) cracked rye
1 cup (120 g) barley grits
½ cup (120 g) Cream of Buckwheat cereal
1 cup (180 g) minced dried apple
¾ cup (135 g) dried tart cherries, dried cranberries, or dried currants
2 teaspoons ground cinnamon

1. In a large bowl, combine all the ingredients; mix well. Store in a covered container or plastic bag at room temperature.

Vanilla Oatmeal Crème Brûlée with Berries

▶ MACHINE: Medium (6-cup [1.4 L]) or large (10-cup) rice cooker; fuzzy logic only ▶ CYCLE: Porridge
▶ YIELD: Serves 4

Crème brûlée oatmeal is the new darling of the bed and breakfast/restaurant brunch set, taking this breakfast staple from rustic to sophisticated. Usually the oatmeal is baked, but here we make individual portions and the cooking is done in the rice cooker. Most recipes contain eggs, but we love this egg-free one. The richly flavored oatmeal is topped with the caramelized sugar crust that is characteristic of the dessert custard of the same name. You can make this in the winter with soaked raisins or dried cranberries and toasted walnuts or almonds in place of the berries. Serve it for company but be prepared, as it is addictive.

1. Place the oats, milk, vanilla, cinnamon, and salt in the rice cooker bowl. Close the cover and set for the Porridge cycle.

2. When the machine switches to the Keep Warm cycle, let the oatmeal steam for 5 minutes. The oatmeal will be semi-thick. With an oversized spoon, fill four 6-ounce (170 g) ramekins, mini soufflé dishes, or custard cups half-full with the oatmeal, then top with a few fresh berries. Spoon the oatmeal over the berries to fill the ramekins to the rim and level each smooth and flat with the back of the spoon. Cool 15 minutes, then cover with plastic wrap and refrigerate until serving time.

3. When ready to serve, preheat the broiler (or you can use a butane kitchen torch). Remove the plastic wrap and place the ramekins on a baking sheet. Combine the two sugars in a small bowl, then sprinkle about 2 teaspoons evenly over the top of each ramekin.

4. Set the pan under the broiler 3 inches (7.5 cm) from the heat until the sugar is melted and starting to bubble and turn amber brown, about 1 minute. Watch carefully to avoid burning. Remove from the oven and let stand for 5 minutes to cool the sugar. Crack the crispy tops and serve topped with more fresh berries and a dollop of yogurt, soy whipped cream, or Cool Whip. Eat out of the ramekin while warm.

1½ cups (120 g) old-fashioned rolled oats (not quick-cooking)

3 cups (700 ml) milk or half-and-half (you can substitute water for part of this) or soy milk

2 teaspoons vanilla extract

¼ teaspoon ground cinnamon

Pinch of salt

About 1 cup (weight will vary) fresh berries of your choice, such as blueberries, blackberries, strawberries, and/or raspberries

2 tablespoons (26 g) granulated sugar

1 tablespoon (15 g) packed light brown sugar

⅔ cup (153 g) plain Greek yogurt, (32 g) soy whipped cream, or (48 g) Cool Whip, for topping

Maple-Cinnamon Rice Pudding

▸ MACHINE: Medium (6-cup [1.4 L]) rice cooker; fuzzy logic only ▸ CYCLE: Porridge ▸ YIELD: Serves 3 to 4

2 cups (372 g) cooked white rice
2½ cups (570 ml) milk
¼ cup (60 ml) heavy cream or milk
¼ cup (60 ml) pure maple syrup
¼ cup (40 g) dried tart cherries, (30 g) dried cranberries, or (35 g) raisins
¼ teaspoon ground cinnamon
Pinch of freshly grated nutmeg
Pinch of fine sea salt

This is a creamy breakfast rice pudding that is perfectly addictive. It can also be made with long-grain brown rice, but the white rice is the creamiest and most nurturing. Serve with pure maple syrup or sliced or chopped fresh or canned fruit, such as bananas, berries, or peaches.

1. The night before serving, combine the rice, milk, cream, maple syrup, dried fruit, spices, and salt in a bowl. Cover and refrigerate until morning.

2. In the morning, coat the rice cooker bowl with butter-flavored nonstick cooking spray. Pour the soaked rice mixture into the rice bowl; stir gently to combine. Close the cover and set for the Porridge cycle.

3. At the end of the cycle, the cereal will be thick and creamy; let it steam on Keep Warm for 10 minutes. Spoon into bowls and serve immediately.

Seven-Herb Rice Porridge (Nanakusagayu)

▶ MACHINE: Medium (6-cup [1.4 L]) or large (10-cup) rice cooker; fuzzy logic only ▶ CYCLE: Porridge
▶ YIELD: Serves 3 to 4

¾ cup (150 g) or 1 rice cooker cup Japanese-style short- or medium-grain rice
4 cups (946 ml) water
1½ cups (weight will vary) mixed dark greens and herbs (see headnote), cores and stems removed, herbs chopped, greens cut into strips no larger than ¼ inch × 2 inches (6 mm × 5 cm)
1 teaspoon salt
1 or 2 eggs (optional)

In Japan, plain rice porridge with seven green herbs is served January 7 as a counterpoint to the New Year's feasting, as well as to bring good health in the year ahead. Japanese supermarkets sell the greens conveniently packaged together just for this porridge; the full list includes turnip and daikon greens as well as five greens lesser known to U.S. cooks. We say just use an assortment of dark green, flavorful greens—spinach, beet greens, parsley, watercress, chard—the number is up to you. The stir-fry blends of baby greens sold loose in better supermarkets are an easy way to get a nice variety of flavors without leftovers

If you choose very tough greens such as collards or kale, you will need to blanch them first. The first time Julie made *nanakusagayu,* her crisper drawer yielded arugula, cilantro, celery leaves, the dark, outer leaves of a head of romaine lettuce, and some beautiful purple-leaved bok choy from her local organic farm subscription box. It was a great combination, as has been every combination we have tried since. Just be sure to cut out cores and tough stems, and chop the greens into strips no bigger than ¼ inch by 2 inches (6 mm × 5 cm).

The traditional New Year version of this dish is just rice, water, salt, and greens, but we like to add 1 or 2 eggs to make a more filling breakfast, lunch, or light supper dish. Refrigerate any leftovers and reheat in the microwave, adding about 2 tablespoons (28 ml) water per serving.

1. Wash the rice. Place the rice in a bowl (or use the bowl of your rice cooker) and fill the bowl about half-full with cold tap water. Swirl the rice in the water with your hand. Carefully pour off most of the water, holding one cupped hand under the stream to catch any grains of rice that are carried away with the water. Holding the bowl steady with one hand, use the other to rub and squeeze the wet rice, turning the bowl as you go, so that all the rice is "scrubbed." The small amount of water in the bowl will turn chalky white. Run cold water into the bowl, give the rice a quick swish, and carefully drain off the water as before.

2. Place the rice and water in the rice cooker bowl; stir gently to combine. Close the cover and set for the Porridge cycle. (If you have time, let the rice soak for 15 to 30 minutes first.)

3. When the machine switches to the Keep Warm cycle, stir in the greens and salt with a wooden or plastic rice paddle or wooden spoon. Close the cover for 1 to 2 minutes to let the greens wilt. Serve immediately. Or, if a heartier dish is desired, beat the egg(s) in a cup. Pour it in a stream over the steamed greens. Close the cover for 2 minutes to let the egg cook a bit. Stir in and serve.

Thanksgiving Jook

▶ MACHINE: Medium (6-cup [1.4 L]) rice cooker; fuzzy logic only   ▶ CYCLE: Porridge   ▶ YIELD: Serves 4 to 6

In fact, you don't really have to wait for Thanksgiving. Julie's friend Grace Liu suggests making it any time a big party leaves you with a turkey or duck carcass, a big ham bone, or some other leftover that is just too good to throw away.

1. Make the stock. Put the carcass into a soup pot, breaking or cutting it into 2 to 4 pieces if necessary to fit. Add the water, using more if necessary so that all or most of the carcass is submerged. Add the onion and ginger. Bring the water to a boil over high heat, cover the pot, and let the stock simmer for 2 hours, until the meat is falling away from the bones. If you are not making jook right away, let the stock cool, uncovered, then cover the pot and refrigerate it for several hours or overnight.

2. When you are ready to make the jook, skim off any fat from the surface of the stock. Strain the stock. Dice or shred 1 cup (140 g) of the turkey meat and reserve it. Discard the rest of the meat. Discard the turkey bones and skin, onion, and ginger.

3. Wash the rice. Place the rice in a bowl (or use the bowl of your rice cooker) and fill the bowl about half-full with cold tap water. Swirl the rice in the water with your hand. Carefully pour off most of the water, holding one cupped hand under the stream to catch any grains of rice that are carried away with the water. Holding the bowl steady with one hand, use the other to rub and squeeze the wet rice, turning the bowl as you go, so that all the rice is "scrubbed." The small amount of water in the bowl will turn chalky white. Now, run cold water into the bowl, give the rice a quick swish, and carefully drain off the water as before. Repeat the scrubbing and pouring-off process two more times. By the third time, the water you pour off will be nearly clear.

4. Place the drained rice in the rice cooker bowl. Add 4½ cups (1.1 L) of the stock, or use a combination of stock and water if there is not enough stock. Add the cabbage and carrot. Close the cover and set for the Porridge cycle.

5. When the machine switches to the Keep Warm cycle, stir in the diced turkey; let the jook steam for 10 minutes. Serve immediately, with any or all of the toppings.

STOCK
1 medium-size turkey carcass
About 12 cups (2.8 L) water
1 small onion, quartered
1 piece (1 inch, or 5 cm) of fresh ginger, cut into 4 pieces and each piece lightly crushed

RICE
¾ cup (150 g) or 1 rice cooker cup Japanese-style short- or medium-grain white rice
2 cups (150 g) shredded Napa cabbage
1 cup (130 g) diced carrot (about 2 medium-size carrots)
Some or all of the following, for topping: sliced green onions, chopped fresh cilantro leaves, peeled and grated fresh ginger, sesame oil, a few drops of soy sauce, salt

BEANS, LEGUMES, and VEGETABLES

Hummus — 137

Frijoles Negros — 138

Italian White Beans — 140

Asparagus with Hollandaise Sauce — 141

Broccoli with Lemon Sauce — 142

Cauliflower with a Puree of Peas — 143

Spiced Yams with Ginger and Pears — 145

Spaghetti Squash Alfredo — 146

Herb and Rice Dolmas — 147

One of the best ways to consume complex carbohydrates, fiber, and vegetable protein in a low-calorie, no-cholesterol package is with beans and legumes. Along with cereal grains, beans are part of our earliest culinary roots, reaching back over 8,000 years. Easily dried for preservation purposes, beans were eaten extensively during long sea voyages and winter months when fresh food was at a premium. They pack a lot of protein into a little package. They are as much a staple today, and for good reason: They are a very versatile food. Beans are notoriously economical: 1 pound (455 g) of dried beans (approximately 2⅓ cups [weight will vary]) will yield about 5 cups [weight will vary] of cooked beans. They tend to show up mostly on winter menus, although that is fast changing; there is nothing quite like a cold cabernet vinegar and olive oil vinaigrette–marinated white bean salad in the summer!

Hummus

▶ MACHINE: Medium (6-cup [1.4 L]) or large (10-cup) rice cooker; fuzzy logic or on/off ▶ CYCLE: Regular
▶ YIELD: 3 cups(738 g); serves 12 as an appetizer

To serve, make a depression in the top of the hummus and drizzle with olive oil until it runs down the sides and pools in the side of the dish. Place spears of romaine lettuce all around for dipping. Give each person a whole fresh pita bread to tear and scoop up this dip.

1. Place the chickpeas in the rice cooker bowl and cover with 3 inches of water. Close the cover, set for the Regular cycle, and set a timer for 1½ hours. During the last half hour of cooking, season with salt to taste.

2. When the timer sounds, test the beans for doneness. Drain the beans, reserving the liquid.

3. In a food processor, finely chop the garlic. Add the warm chickpeas and pulse to mash them. Add the lemon juice, sesame paste, olive oil, and cayenne and, while the machine is running, slowly add ⅓ cup of the reserved cooking liquid through the feed tube until you get a fluffy, smooth consistency. Taste and adjust the flavors.

4. Transfer to a serving bowl and serve immediately, or refrigerate, covered, until ready to serve.

1 cup (200 g) dried chickpeas, picked over, rinsed, soaked in water to cover (overnight or quick-soak method), and drained
Salt
2 to 3 cloves garlic, or more to taste, peeled
¼ to ⅓ cup (60 to 80 ml) fresh lemon juice
⅓ cup (80 g) sesame paste (tahini)
¼ cup (60 ml) extra-virgin olive oil
Pinch of cayenne pepper

Frijoles Negros

▶ MACHINE: Medium (6-cup [1.4 L]) or large (10-cup) rice cooker; fuzzy logic or on/off ▶ CYCLE: Regular
▶ YIELD: About 4 cups; serves 8

1 pound (455 g) dried black beans, picked over, rinsed, soaked in water to cover (overnight or quick-soak method), and drained (about 2 cups)
1 medium-size yellow onion, finely chopped
1 medium-size green or red bell pepper, seeded and finely chopped
1 or 2 fresh jalapeño chiles, seeded and minced
½ teaspoon ground cumin
1 bay leaf
½ cup (123 g) tomato sauce or (130 g) salsa
2 quarts (1.9 L) water
1 tablespoon (15 ml) red wine vinegar
Salt

Black beans, also known as turtle beans, are the cornerstone of Central and South American soul food, just like the pinto bean is in Mexican cooking. Once a specialty item, we now see black beans in every supermarket. They have an appealing, rather addictive, natural flavor and are easy to digest. If you like a smoky edge to your black beans, add two canned chipotle chiles. We like to float a few tablespoons (45 to 60 ml) of olive oil on top of the cooked beans before serving.

1. Place the beans, onion, bell pepper, jalapeño, cumin, bay leaf, tomato sauce or salsa, and water in the rice cooker bowl. Close the cover, set for the Regular cycle, and set a timer for 1½ hours.

2. When the timer sounds, you will have plenty of liquid with the cooked beans. Taste the beans for doneness. Remove the bay leaf. Stir in the vinegar, season with salt to taste, and serve immediately.

Italian White Beans

▶ MACHINE: Medium (6-cup [1.4 L]) or large (10-cup) rice cooker; fuzzy logic or on/off
▶ CYCLE: Quick Cook and/or Regular ▶ YIELD: About 3 cups; serves 6

¼ cup (60 ml) olive oil
1 medium-size yellow on-
  ion, cut into 8 wedges
1 large piece of prosciutto
  rind or 1 small smoked
  ham hock
1 large carrot, cut into thick
  slices
2 stalks celery, with leaves,
  cut into chunks
1 cup (202 g) dried cannellini beans, picked over,
  rinsed, soaked in water
  to cover (overnight or
  quick-soak method), and
  drained
3 cups (700 ml) chicken
  stock
2 bay leaves
Pinch of dried thyme
Salt
Freshly ground black
  pepper

The large oval white kidney bean, also called cannellini, is a favorite home-cooked bean. It has a delicate, sweet flavor and cooks up nice and firm. These beans are a great side dish for fish and meats.

1. Place the olive oil, onion, and meat in the rice cooker bowl. Set the rice cooker for the Quick Cook or Regular cycle and cook for about 15 minutes, stirring a few times. Add the carrot and celery and cook for another 10 minutes to soften slightly, stirring a few times.

2. Add the beans, then add the chicken stock and herbs; stir to combine. Close the cover, reset for the Regular cycle, and set a timer for 1¼ to 1½ hours.

3. When the timer sounds, remove the meat and bay leaves and taste for doneness. Season the beans with salt and pepper to taste and serve immediately.

Asparagus with Hollandaise Sauce

▶ MACHINE: Large (10-cup) rice cooker; on/off only ▶ CYCLE: Regular
▶ YIELD: Serves 5 (1¼ cups [280 g] hollandaise)

This is a classic dish; once you have this version of hollandaise you will never be without a luscious butter sauce again. The sour cream stabilizes it, allowing the sauce to sit in a warm water bath for hours before serving without breaking, or you can make the sauce while the asparagus steams. Use on all sorts of steamed vegetables, including broccoli. The best!

1. Fill the rice cooker bowl about one-quarter full of hot water. Close the cover and set for the Regular cycle.

2. Coat the steamer basket with nonstick cooking spray and place the asparagus in the basket. When the water comes to a boil, place the steamer basket in the cooker and close the cover. Steam until tender, 8 to 15 minutes, depending on the thickness of the stalks.

3. While the asparagus steams, make the sauce. Place the yolks, lemon juice, salt, and pepper in a food processor. Process to combine. With the motor running, add the butter in a slow, steady stream, drop by drop at first, until the sauce is creamy and emulsified. Add the sour cream and pulse to incorporate. Pour the sauce into a heat-resistant deep container. Stand the container in a deep saucepan half-full of hot water over low heat until ready to serve, for 1 to 2 hours.

4. Arrange the asparagus on a serving platter and drizzle with the hollandaise.

2 pounds (900 g) fresh asparagus, bottoms snapped off

HOLLANDAISE SAUCE
4 large egg yolks
1 tablespoon (15 ml) fresh lemon juice
Dash of salt
Dash of ground white pepper
1 cup (2 sticks, or 225 g) unsalted butter, melted and still hot
⅓ cup (77 g) sour cream (Low-fat or IMO imitation sour cream is also acceptable.)

Broccoli with Lemon Sauce

▶ MACHINE: Large (10-cup) rice cooker; on/off only   ▶ CYCLE: Regular   ▶ YIELD: Serves 6

2 pounds (900 g) broccoli, cut into equal-size florets and stems peeled and cut into pieces the size of the florets

LEMON SAUCE
1 small clove of garlic, peeled
1 large egg
2 teaspoons (28 ml) Dijon mustard
2 tablespoons fresh lemon juice
¼ teaspoon salt
Pinch of cayenne pepper
¼ cup (60 ml) olive oil
½ cup (120 ml) canola or vegetable oil

This lemon sauce is really a mayonnaise and a favorite one at that. It is the perfect sauce for fresh broccoli. Once you make homemade mayo, you will understand why this sauce is one of the most beloved in the kitchen. You can substitute orange juice for the lemon. Because the lemon sauce contains raw egg, make sure you use the freshest egg possible, that you keep it refrigerated until ready to serve, and that you eat this the day you make it. Also, because of the possibility of salmonella, it's best not to serve this to small children, the elderly, or anyone with a compromised immune system.

1. Fill the rice cooker bowl about one-quarter full of hot water. Close the cover and set for the Regular cycle.

2. Coat the steamer basket with nonstick cooking spray and place the broccoli in the basket. When the water comes to a boil, place the steamer basket in the cooker and close the cover. Steam until crisp-tender, 12 to 18 minutes.

3. While the broccoli steams, make the Lemon Sauce. In a food processor with the motor running, drop the garlic in through the feed tube to chop. Stop the machine and add the egg, mustard, lemon juice, salt, and cayenne; pulse a few times to combine. With the machine running, slowly drizzle in the oils through the feed tube; the mixture will thicken and be smooth. If you are not using the sauce right away, transfer it to a covered container and refrigerate until ready to serve.

4. Serve small spoonfuls of the Lemon Sauce on the warm broccoli.

Cauliflower with a Puree of Peas

▸ MACHINE: Large (10-cup) rice cooker; on/off only ▸ CYCLE: Regular ▸ YIELD: Serves 6 to 8

If a cauliflower is not perfectly fresh, it can be pretty unappetizing after cooking. So look for a pure creamy head of cauliflower with no spots, which are a sign that it has been around for a while. Sauced with this puree, it is, by our standards, one of the tastiest ways to serve the beautiful flower of the cabbage family. Adapted from one of the best Junior League cookbooks, *San Francisco à la Carte* (Doubleday, 1979).

1. Fill the rice cooker bowl about one-quarter full of hot water. Close the cover and set for the Regular cycle.

2. Coat the steamer basket with nonstick cooking spray and place the cauliflower in the basket. When the water comes to a boil, place the steamer basket in the cooker and close the cover. Steam until tender, 14 to 18 minutes.

3. While the cauliflower steams, make the puree. In a medium-size saucepan, combine the peas, carrots, onions, sugar, thyme, and water. Cook over medium-high heat, partially covered, for 3 minutes. (This can also be done in the top steamer basket, lined with lettuce leaves.) Discard one of the carrots and the onions. Place the peas, the carrots, and the pan juices in a food processor. Add the butter and half-and-half, and process until the mixture is thick and smooth. Season with salt and pepper to taste. Use the puree immediately or transfer to a deep container that can stand in a water bath until serving.

4. Arrange the hot cauliflower on a shallow serving platter, drizzle with the puree, and serve.

1 large or 2 small heads of cauliflower, broken into large florets with 2 inches (5 cm) of stem

PUREE
2 packages (10 ounces, or 280 g each) frozen petite peas
2 small carrots, halved lengthwise
2 green onions
1 tablespoon (13 g) sugar
½ teaspoon dried thyme
¼ cup (60 ml) water
¼ cup (½ stick, or 55 g) unsalted butter
⅓ cup (80 ml) half-and-half
Salt
Freshly ground black pepper

Spiced Yams with Ginger and Pears

▸ MACHINE: Large (10-cup) rice cooker; on/off only ▸ CYCLE: Regular ▸ YIELD: Serves 6

Although yams, as far as we are concerned, are great just plain with butter, here is one step beyond in case you need a special holiday dish. The pears give it a lot of sweetness, so balance with another vegetable, such as green beans or zucchini, in your menu.

1. Preheat the oven to 350°F (180°C, or gas mark 4). Fill the rice cooker bowl about one-quarter full of hot water. Close the cover and set for the Regular cycle.

2. Coat the steamer basket with nonstick cooking spray and place the yams in the basket. When the water comes to a boil, place the steamer basket in the cooker and close the cover. Steam until soft enough to mash, 10 to 15 minutes.

3. Transfer the yams to a large bowl. With a fork, coarsely mash the yams with the ginger, cardamom, and salt. Fold in the pears. Spoon into a shallow 1½-quart (1.4 L) gratin dish and smooth the top. (At this point, you can cover the dish and refrigerate for up to 4 hours.) Bake until heated through, 15 to 20 minutes. Serve immediately.

2 pounds (900 g) ruby yams or sweet potatoes, peeled and cut into 2-inch (5 cm) chunks

2 teaspoons peeled and grated fresh ginger

1 teaspoon ground cardamom

Pinch of salt

3 firm ripe pears, peeled, cored, diced, and drizzled with the juice of 1 small lemon to prevent discoloration

Spaghetti Squash Alfredo

▸ MACHINE: Large (10-cup) rice cooker; on/off only ▸ CYCLE: Regular ▸ YIELD: Serves 2

1 spaghetti squash (2 to 2½ pounds [900 g to 1.1 kg])
2 tablespoons (28 g) unsalted butter
⅓ cup (80 ml) heavy cream
½ cup (50 g) freshly grated Parmesan cheese
2 fresh basil leaves, cut into thin strips
Salt
Freshly ground black pepper

Beth learned this recipe in the 1980s from Louise's Pantry Cooking School in Menlo Park, California. Spaghetti squash had just hit the market and no one knew quite what to do with the football-shaped squash with a stringy interior. People who are allergic to wheat and can't eat pasta go for this rendition in a big way. Steaming is the best way to cook this squash that ends up looking so very much like spaghetti, so the delicate insides don't get mushy. Spaghetti squash is also good with a tomato vinaigrette, or mixed with half spinach and half plain angel hair pasta.

1. Fill the rice cooker bowl about one-quarter full of hot water. Close the cover and set for the Regular cycle.

2. Meanwhile, wash the squash and halve with a cleaver or large, heavy knife. Scoop out the seeds and fibers. Halve each piece again.

3. Coat the steamer basket with nonstick cooking spray and place the squash cut-side down in the basket. When the water comes to a boil, place the steamer basket in the cooker and close the cover. Steam until your finger leaves an indentation when pressed into the squash, 20 to 30 minutes.

4. Remove the basket from the cooker. Gently pull the strands from the shell with a large spoon until only the thin skin remains. Place the squash in a warm serving bowl and toss with the butter, cream, cheese, basil, and salt and pepper to taste. Serve immediately.

Herb and Rice Dolmas

▶ MACHINE: Large (10-cup) rice cooker; on/off or fuzzy logic ▶ CYCLE: Quick Cook and/or Regular
▶ YIELD: 28 dolmas; serves 6 to 8 as an appetizer

While many dolma fillings contain lamb or lentils, this recipe has a great rice, vegetable, herb, goat cheese, fruit, and nut filling. No matter what filling you decide on, this is the basic procedure to use for preparing the grape leaves and filling and steaming them.

1. Place the rice in a fine strainer or bowl, rinse with cold water two to four times, and drain. The water will be chalky and slightly foamy. Spread the wet rice out with your hands on a clean tea towel on the counter. Let air-dry for at least 1 hour, until cooking time.

2. Make the rice: Set the rice cooker for the Quick Cook or Regular cycle. Place the olive oil in the rice cooker bowl. When hot, add the onion and garlic and cook, stirring a few times, until softened, about 2 minutes. Add the rice and cook, stirring, until all the grains are evenly coated and hot. Add the water, salt, cinnamon stick, and currants; stir just to combine. Close the cover and reset for the Regular cycle or let the Regular cycle complete. When the machine switches to the Keep Warm cycle, let the rice steam for 10 minutes.

3. Rinse the grape leaves under cold running water and drain on layers of paper towels. With kitchen shears, cut off the stems. Set aside.

4. Open the cover, remove the rice cooker bowl, discard the cinnamon stick, and fluff the rice with a wooden or plastic rice paddle or wooden spoon. Stir in the parsley, mint, lemon zest, and pine nuts.

(Continued on next page)

RICE
¾ cup (135 g) basmati rice
3 tablespoons (45 ml) olive oil
1 small yellow onion, finely chopped
1 clove of garlic, minced
1 cup (235 ml) water
Pinch of salt
1 cinnamon stick (4 inches, or 10 cm)
¼ cup (38 g) dried currants
2 tablespoons (8 g) minced fresh Italian parsley leaves
1 tablespoon minced fresh mint leaves or dill
Grated zest of ½ of a small lemon
3 tablespoons (27 g) pine nuts or (19 g) chopped blanched almonds, toasted

DOLMAS
1 jar (8 to 10 ounces, or 225 to 280 g) preserved grape leaves
5 ounces (140 g) goat cheese
2 cups (475 ml) water
2 tablespoons (28 ml) olive oil
¼ cup (60 ml) fresh lemon juice

Lemon wedges or cold plain yogurt, for serving

5. Make the dolmas: To fill, place a perfect leaf, shiny side down, rib side up, on your work surface. Place a tablespoon (15 ml) of the rice mixture and a piece of goat cheese (about ½ teaspoon) on top in the center of the leaf. Fold the sides in as for an envelope and roll up jelly-roll fashion to make a small, plump cylinder. If you have any tears, snip off a lobe and patch from the inside. Fill all the leaves in the same fashion. You will have enough filling for about 28 leaves.

6. Wash and dry the rice cooker bowl and return it to the machine body. Spray with nonstick cooking spray and line with the extra grape leaves, in an overlapping pattern. Place the dolmas in a single layer, seam side down and close side by side, on the bed of grape leaves. Add a second layer of dolmas.

7. In a measuring cup, combine the water, olive oil, and lemon juice. Pour over the dolmas in the rice cooker; the liquid should not come more than halfway up the sides (you may have extra). Close the cover and set for the Regular cycle. After the cooking liquid comes to a simmer, cook the dolmas until they are firm to the touch and the leaf is tender when cut in half, 20 to 25 minutes.

8. Remove the cover carefully and let the dolmas cool slightly.

9. Serve the dolmas warm or at room temperature, with lemon wedges or plain yogurt. Or let them cool, place in a flat covered container, refrigerate overnight, and serve chilled or at room temperature.

WHOLE-MEAL STEAMING

Steamed Chicken Breasts on Wild Rice with Gingered Tomato Relish — 151

Steamed Chicken Breasts with Warm Mango Sauce and Coconut Rice — 154

Steamed Salmon Steaks with Pineapple Salsa — 155

Steamed Sausages and Sauerkraut with Champagne — 156

Steamed Shrimp and Jasmine Rice — 157

Once you get comfortable using the steamer tray and baskets of your on/off rice cooker for vegetables, the next step is to create whole meals in the unit. Cuisines that utilize steam all have full-course steamed meals that are low in fat and quite quick to prepare. Rice (especially sticky short-grain *japonicas*) is traditionally steamed in a basket over hot water. Indian brass or tin steamers allow a full meal to be made at one time: the dal in the bottom bowl, the vegetables in the first level, and the basmati steamed on top. The simplicity of it all is ingenious. It is an addictively convenient form of cooking and if you have limited space, you will adore it and end up creating your own versions. If you use the tiered plastic baskets, you can even carry them to the table (with the lid on!) and serve or eat directly from them.

Steamed Chicken Breasts on Wild Rice with Gingered Tomato Relish

▶ MACHINE: Medium (6-cup) and large (10-cup) rice cookers; on/off only ▶ CYCLE: Regular ▶ YIELD: Serves 4

Although this recipe employs two rice cookers, it is terribly simple, which is why it gets made so often. Originally a "gourmet-lite" recipe from former Sonoma Mission Inn chef Larry Elbert using broiled chicken breast, the recipe made the leap perfectly for the chicken breast to be marinated and steamed. A steamed chicken breast is wonderfully tender and juicy. Use this recipe as a basic one; if you don't have time to marinate, just wash the breast in lots of fresh lemon juice and a tablespoon (15 ml) of olive oil. Serve on a bed of plain, fresh cooked wild rice, with a bit of the tomato relish on top.

1. Make the marinade: Place the marinade ingredients in a shallow bowl; whisk to combine. Place the chicken, skin side up, in the marinade. Cover and refrigerate for at least 2 hours.

2. Make the Gingered Tomato Relish: Place the relish ingredients in a small bowl; stir to combine. Cover and refrigerate until serving.

3. Make the rice: Place the wild rice in the rice cooker bowl of a medium (6-cup [1.4 L]) or large (10-cup) rice cooker. Add the water and salt; swirl to combine. Close the cover and set for the Regular cycle. When the machine switches to the Keep Warm cycle, stir with a wooden or plastic rice paddle or wooden spoon to dissipate the heat and prevent overcooking. Close the cover and let the rice steam for 10 minutes. This step will take close to 1 hour, so plan accordingly.

(Continued on next page)

MARINADE AND CHICKEN
⅓ cup (80 g) Dijon mustard
3 tablespoons (45 ml) red wine vinegar
3 tablespoons (45 ml) fresh lemon juice
1 clove of garlic, pressed
1½ teaspoons herbes de Provence or dried basil leaves, crumbled
⅔ cup (160 ml) olive oil or vegetable oil
4 boneless chicken breast halves, with skin on

GINGERED TOMATO RELISH
2 medium-size ripe tomatoes, blanched for a few seconds in boiling water, peeled, seeds squeezed out, and diced
3 tablespoons (18 g) chopped green onions, white and green parts
1 tablespoon (15 ml) extra-virgin olive oil
1 tablespoon (15 ml) champagne vinegar
½ teaspoon peeled and grated fresh ginger
Splash of Tabasco sauce
Pinch of salt or nonsalt alternative, such as Spike Vegit

WILD RICE
1¼ cups (200 g) wild rice
2¾ cups (650 ml) water
Pinch of salt
2 to 3 large chard leaves, stems discarded, or Napa cabbage leaves, for lining steamer basket (optional)

Steamed Chicken Breasts on Wild Rice with Gingered Tomato Relish, *continued*

4. Fill a large (10-cup, [2.4 L]) rice cooker bowl one-quarter full of hot water, close the cover, and set for the Regular cycle. Line one steamer tray or basket with a single layer of chard or cabbage leaves or a piece of parchment paper. Remove the chicken from the marinade and arrange on the steamer tray or basket. If you are having steamed vegetables with the chicken (like some zucchini), you can arrange them in the top tier if you are using baskets. When the water comes to a boil, place the tray or basket in the cooker and close the cover. Set a timer and steam for 20 to 25 minutes. Check the chicken for doneness; it should no longer be pink in the center.

5. To serve, divide the rice among four dinner plates, place a chicken breast on top, and spoon some Gingered Tomato Relish in a mound on top. Serve immediately.

Steamed Chicken Breasts with Warm Mango Sauce and Coconut Rice

▶ MACHINE: Large (10-cup [2.4 L]) rice cooker; on/off only ▶ CYCLE: Regular ▶ YIELD: Serves 4

2½ cups (450 g) basmati rice or other aromatic long-grain rice, such as jasmine or Jasmati

2 cans (14-ounces, or 410 g each) unsweetened coconut milk (can be light)

¼ cup (60 ml) water

⅛ teaspoon salt (optional)

4 boneless, skinless chicken breast halves

1 pound (455 g) thick asparagus spears, tough bottoms discarded, and/or 2 chayote squashes, peeled, seeded, halved, and cut into 1½-inch-(3.8 cm) thick slices

WARM MANGO SAUCE

1 large ripe mango, peeled, seeded, and cut into neat ½-inch (1.3 cm) pieces

¼ cup (60 ml) dry white wine

2 tablespoons (28 ml) rice vinegar

2 tablespoons (26 g) sugar

2 teaspoons peeled and minced fresh ginger

⅛ teaspoon ground allspice

Salt

Freshly ground black pepper

3 tablespoons (3 g) minced fresh cilantro leaves, for garnish

This is a chicken recipe contributed by our local Mexican food expert and cooking teacher Marge Poore, the author of *365 Easy Mexican Recipes* (HarperCollins, 1997) and *1,000 Mexican Recipes* (HarperCollins, 2001). She also leads very popular food tours of Mexico. Here Poore combines tropical mangos with steamed chicken breasts and we couldn't be more excited about the combination. We serve this dish from the steamer baskets with coconut rice and steamed asparagus and/or chayote squash, a vegetable that often is served steamed or sautéed as a side vegetable in Mexico.

1. Rinse the rice in a fine strainer until the water runs clear. Place the rice in the rice cooker bowl. Add the coconut milk, water, and salt, if using; swirl to combine.

2. Coat the steamer baskets with nonstick cooking spray and arrange the chicken in one basket. Place the asparagus and/or chayote in the other basket or arrange it around the chicken. Place the steamer baskets in the rice cooker. Close the cover and set for the Regular cycle.

3. Make the Mango Sauce: In a medium-size saucepan, combine the mango, wine, vinegar, sugar, ginger, and allspice. Bring to a boil over medium heat, stirring to dissolve the sugar. Reduce the heat to low and simmer, uncovered, for 5 minutes. Remove from the heat and set aside.

4. When the machine switches to the Keep Warm cycle, check to make sure the chicken is no longer pink inside and the vegetables are tender. Fluff the rice with a wooden or plastic rice paddle or wooden spoon.

5. To serve, transfer the rice to a serving platter and top with the chicken. Arrange the vegetables around the rice and season with salt and pepper to taste. Reheat the Mango Sauce and spoon a small amount over the chicken. Garnish with cilantro. Pass the remaining Mango Sauce at the table.

Steamed Salmon Steaks with Pineapple Salsa

▶ MACHINE: Large (10-cup [2.4 L]) rice cooker; on/off only ▶ CYCLE: Regular ▶ YIELD: Serves 4

Salmon steaks, now readily available because of farm-raised fish, are a sure thing for a fast dinner. This marinade is wonderful; we keep sake around just for this. Serve with some hot jasmine rice.

1. Make the marinade: Place the marinade ingredients in a shallow bowl; whisk to combine. Place the salmon in the marinade, coating both sides well. Cover and refrigerate for 1 to 2 hours, turning once.

2. Make the Pineapple Salsa: Place the salsa ingredients in a small bowl; stir to combine. Cover and refrigerate until serving.

3. Fill the rice cooker bowl one-quarter full of hot water, close the cover, and set for the Regular cycle.

4. Line the steamer baskets with a single layer of chard or cabbage leaves or a piece of parchment paper. Remove the salmon steaks from the marinade and arrange on one or two tiers of the steamer basket. (If you are steaming vegetables with the salmon, you can arrange them around the sides of the tiers.) When the water comes to a boil, place the steamer baskets in the cooker and close the cover. Set a timer and steam for 18 to 23 minutes. Check for doneness; the fish should be opaque and firm.

5. Serve the salmon immediately, with the Pineapple Salsa.

MARINADE AND SALMON
¾ cup (175 ml) dry sake
¾ cup (175 ml) reduced-sodium soy sauce
⅓ cup (67 g) sugar
4 salmon steaks (6 to 8 ounces, or 170 to 225 g), ¾ inch (1.9 cm) thick

PINEAPPLE SALSA
1½ cups (235 g) diced fresh pineapple
⅓ cup (100 g) seeded and minced red bell pepper
¼ cup (40 g) minced red onion
¼ cup (4 g) minced fresh cilantro leaves
Juice and grated zest of 1 large lime
2½ teaspoons (5 g) seeded and minced jalapeño chile
2 to 3 large chard leaves, stems discarded, or Napa cabbage leaves, for lining steamer basket (optional)

Steamed Shrimp and Jasmine Rice

▶ MACHINE: Medium (6-cup) or large (10-cup) rice cooker; on/off only ▶ CYCLE: Regular ▶ YIELD: Serves 4

1⅓ cups (240 g) Thai jasmine rice
2⅔ cups (635 ml) water
Pinch of salt
8 green onions, trimmed to fit steaming tray
1 pound (455 g) medium-size shrimp, shelled (tails left on) and deveined
2 pinches of dillweed
Ground white pepper
Sprigs of fresh Italian parsley, basil, or sage, for garnish

Shrimp is an excellent seafood for the rice cooker because it cooks so quickly. If your cooker has a glass lid, it's easy to tell when the shrimp are cooked by their bright orange-pink color; if you have to lift the lid to check the shrimp, do so with care to avoid the steam. If the shrimp is finished before the end of the rice cooking cycle, carefully remove the shrimp and green onions, either by removing the whole steaming tray or by transferring the ingredients with a spatula or tongs.

Timing this recipe takes a little practice, but the whole dish couldn't be easier. Chopping up and mixing in the steamed green onions gives great flavor and texture to the cooked rice. You might try this with baby leeks instead of green onions. This is a light meal, suitable for lunch or Sunday night supper. This recipe comes from the kitchen of our literary agent, Martha Casselman.

1. Rinse the rice. Place it in the rice cooker bowl with the water and salt; swirl to combine. Close the cover and set for the Regular cycle.

2. Place the green onions on the steamer tray and lay the shrimp on top in a single layer. Sprinkle with the dillweed and white pepper to season.

3. About 8 minutes before the end of the Regular cycle (depending on brand and size, about 15 minutes into the cycle), place the steaming tray in the cooker and close the cover. Steam the shrimp for about 6 minutes, until the color has changed to orange-pink. Do not overcook the shrimp, or they will become tough. Remove the steaming tray and place the shrimp in a warm covered dish. Let the onions cool, then chop them enough to stir them into the rice when it is done; you will have about ⅓ cup (33 g).

4. When the machine switches to the Keep Warm cycle, stir the green onions into the rice with a plastic or wooden rice paddle or wooden spoon.

5. To serve, mound the rice on a serving platter or four individual plates, place the shrimp on top, and garnish with the herb sprigs.

Steamed Sausages and Sauerkraut with Champagne

▶ MACHINE: Large (10-cup [2.4 L]) rice cooker; on/off only ▶ CYCLE: Regular ▶ YIELD: Serves 4

2½ to 3 pounds (1.1 to 1.4 kg) sauerkraut, rinsed

⅓ cup (80 ml) dry champagne or sparkling white wine

8 fully cooked sausages, such as smoked chicken-apple or bockwurst with chives

12 medium-size red or white new potatoes, cut in half or quarters, or 24 baby creamer potatoes, left whole and unpeeled

¼ cup (½ stick, or 55 g) unsalted butter, for serving

2 teaspoons dillweed, for serving

With the advent of the healthier sausages, it is now easy to eat them once a week. Here is an incredibly easy entrée. The amount of sauerkraut depends on your diners; anyone from Europe will eat a hearty serving. You can brown the sausages first in a skillet if you like, but that is optional. Serve with a variety of mustards and some butter and dillweed on the potatoes. We like to serve it with a tossed salad with sliced cucumbers or cole slaw.

1. Fill the rice cooker bowl one-quarter full of hot water, close the cover, and set for the Regular cycle.

2. Line two steamer baskets with a single sheet of parchment paper each. Divide the sauerkraut in half and arrange it like a bed in the center of both baskets; drizzle with the champagne. Place 4 sausages on each bed of sauerkraut, then loosely arrange the potatoes around the sauerkraut. When the water comes to a boil, place the baskets in the cooker and close the cover. Set a timer and steam for 30 to 40 minutes. Check for doneness: The potatoes should be tender when pierced with the tip of a knife and the sausages nice and hot.

3. Serve immediately, with each diner having 2 sausages, sauerkraut, and some potatoes with 1 tablespoon (14 g) butter and ½ teaspoon dillweed sprinkled on.

PUDDINGS, CUSTARDS, and FRUIT DESSERTS

Coconut Tapioca Pudding — 161

Old-Fashioned Rice Pudding — 161

Tres Leches Rice Pudding — 162

Brown Rice Kheer (Indian Rice Pudding) — 163

Poached Rhubarb and Strawberries — 165

Poached Fresh Cherries — 165

Steamed Chocolate Custards — 166

English Pudding with Cranberries and Walnuts — 169

Steamed Lemon Custards — 170

English Custard Sauce — 170

While we often think of rice as just a dinner side dish or in rice pudding for dessert, rice is so beloved that an old-fashioned dessert of European royalty was to eat freshly steamed plain long-grain rice with spoonfuls of cherry or strawberry preserves and whipped cream or sour cream on top.

The Porridge cycle on the fuzzy logic machines, with its gentle, even heat source, makes beautiful, creamy, sweet dessert puddings such as tapioca and rice pudding, delightful desserts that have starch at their heart. It also makes lovely fruit desserts such as applesauce, compotes, and poached fruit. This is pure comfort food, softly cooked, warm, sweet. These are not elaborate desserts, just soothing simplicity. The Porridge cycle is essential to the success of these recipes. Please note that these recipes cannot be made in the on/off machines because the heat is just too high.

Coconut Tapioca Pudding

▶ MACHINE: Medium (6-cup [1.4 L]) rice cooker; fuzzy logic only ▶ CYCLE: Porridge ▶ YIELD: Serves 6

We knew tapioca pudding from childhood as "fish eye pudding." Here it is made with a twist, coconut milk instead of regular milk, just like it would be prepared in Thailand. Try to use small pearl tapioca beads, not instant tapioca, which is very small and jells up very fast. (If you do make this with instant tapioca, reduce the amount to ¼ cup [48 g].) We like Cook's Cookie vanilla extract; it is a combination of vanillas that is especially flowery and delicate in flavor. Coconut-based puddings are nice with some chopped tropical fruit, such as pineapple or mango, on top.

> 3¼ cups (760 ml) canned unsweetened coconut milk
> ¾ cup (132 g) small pearl tapioca
> ¾ cup (150 g) sugar
> 1 large egg
> Pinch of salt
> 2½ teaspoons (13 ml) pure vanilla extract, preferably Tahitian

1. Place the coconut milk, tapioca, sugar, egg, and salt in the rice cooker bowl; stir to combine. Close the cover and set for the Porridge cycle. Open the cover and stir about every 20 minutes for a few seconds, then close the cover.

2. When the machine switches to the Keep Warm cycle, remove the bowl from the cooker and stir in the vanilla. Pour the pudding into a large bowl or individual dessert dishes. Let cool. Serve warm, if desired, or refrigerate, covered with plastic wrap.

Old-Fashioned Rice Pudding

▶ MACHINE: Medium (6-cup [1.4 L]) rice cooker; fuzzy logic only ▶ CYCLE: Porridge ▶ YIELD: Serves 6

Here is the quintessential rice pudding of everyone's childhood. It is sweet and creamy, no fancy or exotic ingredients. Whole milk is best, but 2 percent works fine. It is slowly simmered in the rice cooker and ready to eat as soon as it cools. Remember that rice pudding thickens considerably when chilled as the starch in the rice sets up.

> ⅔ cup (130 g) medium-grain white rice, such as Arborio, Calriso, or other California-grown rice
> 4 cups (946 ml) milk
> 1 large egg
> ⅓ cup (67 g) sugar
> 1 teaspoon pure vanilla extract

1. Place the rice and milk in the rice cooker bowl; stir to combine. Close the cover and set for the Porridge cycle.

2. When the machine switches to the Keep Warm cycle, combine the egg, sugar, and vanilla in a small bowl and beat with a whisk. Open the rice cooker, spoon a few tablespoons (45 to 60 ml) of the rice milk into the egg mixture, and beat with a wooden spoon. Beating the rice milk constantly, pour the rest of the egg mixture into the rice cooker bowl. Stir for a minute to combine. Close the cover and reset for a second Porridge cycle. Stir every 15 to 20 minutes until the desired thickness is reached.

3. Pour the pudding into 6 custard cups or ramekins. Serve warm or let cool slightly and refrigerate for at least 1 hour. When cold, cover with plastic wrap and store for up to 4 days.

Tres Leches Rice Pudding

▸ MACHINE: Medium (6-cup [1.4 L]) rice cooker; fuzzy logic or on/off ▸ CYCLE: Regular and/or Porridge
▸ YIELD: Serves 4

1½ cups (270 g) Arborio rice or other short-grain rice (see headnote)

2 cups (475 ml) water

½ teaspoon salt

½ cup (120 ml) evaporated milk

⅔ cup (160 ml) unsweetened coconut milk (Don't shake the can, use the top cream.)

1 cup (235 ml) sweetened condensed milk, organic preferred

1½ teaspoons pure vanilla extract

½ teaspoon freshly grated nutmeg

1 cinnamon stick

1 strip (3 to 4 inches, or 7.5 to 10 cm) of lemon zest (Cut around the whole lemon for one long, wide strip.)

You can make this egg-free rice pudding with a number of glutinous rices, such as Italian Arborio, Vialono nano, Japanese Tamaki *haiga mai,* Lundberg Sweet Brown Rice, or a black rice like Chinese Forbidden Rice or Italian *riso nero* (the hybrid of Arborio and Forbidden rice grown in northern Italy). Serve with whipped cream.

1. Place the rice in a fine strainer or bowl, and rinse with cold water until the water runs clear.

2. Place the rice, water, and salt in the rice cooker bowl. Close the cover and set for the Regular cycle.

3. When the machine switches to the Keep Warm cycle, stir in the evaporated, coconut, and condensed milks, vanilla, and nutmeg. Submerge the cinnamon stick and lemon zest. Reset for the Porridge cycle. (If the cycle doesn't start immediately, disconnect the cord from the outlet, let stand 15 minutes, then plug back in and reset the cycle.)

4. When the machine switches to the Keep Warm cycle for a second time, open the cover and let the pudding cool at room temperature, uncovered, for about 20 minutes, stirring occasionally to prevent a skin from forming on the surface. Discard the cinnamon stick and zest strip. Serve warm or transfer to a covered glass bowl and refrigerate until chilled.

Brown Rice Kheer (Indian Rice Pudding)

▶ MACHINE: Medium (6-cup [1.4 L]) rice cooker; fuzzy logic only   ▶ CYCLE: Porridge   ▶ YIELD: Serves 8 to 10

⅔ cup (120 g) brown
   basmati rice
4½ cups (1.1 L) whole milk
½ cup (100 g) raw sugar
3 tablespoons (21 g) slivered almonds
4 green cardamom pods
2 tablespoons (23 g) white
   basmati rice
4 to 5 saffron strands

While we love the creamy, sweet *kheer* in the preceding recipe, we wanted to give it a healthful makeover. This recipe is the result. We used two tricks to coax the normally chewy brown basmati into a pudding. First, we extended the cooking time by using two back-to-back Porridge cycles. Second, we added a very small amount (just 2 tablespoons [23 g]) of white basmati before starting the second cycle. The white basmati helps provide the familiar, creamy background. We also added heart-healthy almonds, reduced the sugar, and eliminated the cream. *Kheer* lovers will be able to tell the difference between our "spa" *kheer* and *kheer* made with all white rice, but we like the post-makeover pudding, too.

1. Gently wash the brown rice. Place the rice in a bowl (or use the bowl of your rice cooker) and fill the bowl about half-full with cold tap water. Swirl the rice in the water with your hand. Carefully pour off the water.

2. Place the brown rice, milk, sugar, almonds, and cardamom in the rice cooker bowl. Stir briefly with a wooden or plastic rice paddle or wooden spoon. Close the cover and set for the Porridge cycle.

3. When the machine switches to the Keep Warm cycle, stir in the white rice and saffron. Reset for a second Porridge cycle.

4. When the machine switches to the Keep Warm cycle for a second time, open the cover and remove the bowl. Let the kheer cool at room temperature, uncovered, for about 30 minutes, stirring occasionally to prevent a skin from forming on the surface. Discard the cardamom pods.

5. Serve warm or transfer the pudding to a serving bowl and cover tightly with plastic wrap. Chill in the refrigerator and serve cool or nice and cold.

Poached Rhubarb and Strawberries

▶ MACHINE: Large (10-cup) rice cooker; fuzzy logic only ▶ CYCLE: Porridge ▶ YIELD: About 4 cups

Don't have time to make a strawberry-rhubarb pie? Well, this early summer fresh fruit compote has all the flavor and pretty color without any of the fuss. Note that the recipe says to be careful with the stirring, so that the fruits do not get stringy and mushy. The flavor is so very delightful and especially good with vanilla gelato.

1 cup (235 ml) water
1 cup (200 g) sugar
1 vanilla bean, split
1 pound (455 g) fresh rhubarb stems, cut into
   1½-inch (3.8 cm) chunks (about 4 cups [488 g])
1½ pints (510 g) fresh strawberries, rinsed, hulled,
   and halved

1. Place the water, sugar, vanilla bean, and rhubarb in the rice cooker bowl. Close the cover and set for the Porridge cycle. Set a timer for 30 minutes; when the timer sounds, add the strawberries and stir once to distribute. Close the cover and let the cycle complete.

2. When the machine switches to the Keep Warm cycle, carefully open the cover, remove the bowl from the cooker, and let cool. Do not stir. Serve the compote warm or at room temperature, or pour into a storage container, cover, and refrigerate overnight to serve chilled, ladled into dessert bowls. Keeps for up to 4 days in the refrigerator.

Poached Fresh Cherries

▶ MACHINE: Large (10-cup) rice cooker; fuzzy logic only ▶ CYCLE: Porridge ▶ YIELD: 4 cups

Is there anyone who doesn't love cherries? While the season for fresh cherries is, sadly, very short and the large orchards of the past are on the wane, cherries still are the most coveted of fruits, whether in jam, pies, or this compote, because of their exceptionally flavorful pulp.

3 cups (700 ml) cranberry-raspberry or
   unsweetened cherry juice
1 cup (235 ml) water
⅔ cup (133 g) sugar
1 tablespoon (15 ml) pure vanilla extract
2 pounds (900 g) sweet cherries, stems removed
   and pitted

1. Place all the ingredients in the rice cooker bowl. Close the cover and set for the Porridge cycle. Set a timer for 30 minutes. Check the consistency of the cherries at 30 minutes by piercing their flesh with the tip of a small knife; you want them firm, but slightly tender. Remember, they will soften a bit more as they cool.

2. When the cherries are the desired consistency, remove the bowl from the cooker. Transfer the cherries and their poaching liquid to a storage container and let cool. Cover and refrigerate for at least 4 hours and up to overnight. Serve chilled, with some of the liquid. Keeps for up to 3 days in the refrigerator.

Steamed Chocolate Custards

▶ MACHINE: Large (10-cup) rice cooker; on/off only ▶ CYCLE: Regular ▶ YIELD: Serves 4

1½ cups (355 ml) whole milk
½ cup (88 g) semisweet chocolate chips
2 tablespoons (10 g) Dutch-process unsweetened cocoa powder, such as Droste
¼ cup (60 g) firmly packed dark brown sugar
Pinch of salt
1 large egg
2 large egg yolks
½ teaspoon pure vanilla extract

This is a delectable chocolate custard that begs for some whipped cream on top.

1. Coat the inside of 4 custard cups or ramekins with butter-flavored nonstick cooking spray.

2. In a small saucepan, whisk together the milk, chocolate chips, and cocoa over medium heat just until the chocolate melts, stirring occasionally.

3. In a medium-size bowl, combine the brown sugar and salt. Whisk in the whole egg, egg yolks, and vanilla until smooth. Whisk in about a quarter of the chocolate mixture, beating vigorously. Slowly pour in the remaining chocolate mixture in a steady stream, whisking constantly to avoid curdling. Pour the custard into the prepared custard cups. Cover each cup with a small square of aluminum foil and crimp the edges to seal airtight.

4. Add 4 cups (946 ml) of hot water to the rice cooker bowl, close the cover, and set for the Regular cycle. When the water comes to a boil, arrange the cups in the tray or baskets (this works best steaming a double rack of custards at one time). Place the tray or baskets in the cooker and close the cover. Steam until the custards are just set and slightly wobbly in the center, 35 to 40 minutes. Unplug the machine to turn it off.

5. Remove each custard of from the rice cooker with metal tongs. Remove the foil covers. Let cool and then serve at room temperature or refrigerate until ready to serve.

English Pudding with Cranberries and Walnuts

▶ MACHINE: Large (10-cup) rice cooker; on/off only ▶ CYCLE: Regular ▶ YIELD: Serves 8 to 10

This is an Americanized version of the very traditional, very beloved English pudding called *spotted dick*, which originally called for shredded suet and raisins. Serve with a package of Bird's custard sauce made according to the package instructions, if you want to be very English, or else use the following recipe for old-fashioned English Custard Sauce.

1. Set up the rice cooker for steaming by placing a small trivet or wire cooling rack in the bottom of the rice bowl. Fill the bowl one-quarter to one-third full of hot water, close the cover, and set for the Regular cycle. If the water boils before you are ready to steam the pudding, flip the switch to the Keep Warm position (switch back for cooking). Generously grease or coat the inside of a 1½-quart (6-cup, or 1.4 L) round melon-shaped tin pudding mold with a clip-on lid with butter-flavored nonstick cooking spray.

2. In a large bowl, combine all the ingredients (except the English Custard Sauce) in the order given with a large rubber spatula. Stir well with a folding motion until evenly moistened.

3. Scrape the batter into the prepared mold, filling it two-thirds full; snap on the lid. Set the mold on the trivet or wire rack in the bottom of the cooker, making sure it is centered and not tipped. Close the cover and reset the cooker for the Regular cycle to bring back to a rolling boil, if necessary. Set a timer and steam for 1 hour, checking a few times to be sure the water doesn't boil off. Check the pudding for doneness; it should feel slightly firm to the touch, yet slightly moist. It should be puffed, rising to fill the mold, and a cake tester inserted in the center should come out clean. Unplug the machine to turn it off.

4. Using oven mitts, carefully transfer the mold from the steamer to a wire rack and remove the lid. Let stand for a few minutes, then turn upside down to unmold the pudding onto the rack or a serving plate.

5. Serve still warm, cut into wedges, or at room temperature, with English Custard Sauce, if you like.

½ cup (120 ml) hot water
½ cup (170 g) light molasses
2 teaspoons baking soda
¼ teaspoon salt
¼ teaspoon ground ginger
¼ teaspoon ground cinnamon
1½ cups (188 g) all-purpose flour (Beth uses White Lily bleached all-purpose flour, a southern favorite, unsifted right out of the bag.)
2 cups (200 g) fresh or (220 g) frozen (and thawed) cranberries
½ cup (60 g) chopped walnuts
English Custard Sauce (recipe follows; optional)

Steamed Lemon Custards

▸ MACHINE: Large (10-cup) rice cooker; on/off only ▸ CYCLE: Regular ▸ YIELD: Serves 4

We love this custard! Use an organic heavy cream, if you can, and the sumptuous pure citrus oils from Boyajian; the flavors are the edible perfume of the food world. You can find them in large supermarkets and gourmet stores.

1 cup (235 ml) heavy cream
¼ cup (50 g) sugar
2 large eggs
2 large egg yolks
1 teaspoon lemon oil or pure lemon extract

1. Coat the inside of 4 custard cups or ramekins with butter-flavored nonstick cooking spray.

2. In a small, deep bowl, beat together all the ingredients with a whisk or handheld immersion blender until well blended. Pour the custard into the prepared custard cups. Cover each cup with a small square of aluminum foil and crimp the edges to seal airtight.

3. Add 4 cups (946 ml) of hot water to the rice cooker bowl, close the cover, and set for the Regular cycle. When the water comes to a boil, arrange the cups in the tray or baskets (this works best steaming a double rack of custards at one time). Place the tray or baskets in the cooker and close the cover. Steam until the custards are just set and slightly wobbly in the center, 35 to 40 minutes. Unplug the machine to turn it off.

4. Remove each pudding from the rice cooker with metal tongs. Remove the foil covers. Let cool, then refrigerate until ready to serve.

English Custard Sauce

▸ YIELD: 2 cups

2 cups (475 ml) whole milk
¼ cup (50 g) sugar
1 teaspoon cornstarch
5 large egg yolks
1½ teaspoons pure vanilla extract or 1½ table-spoons (25 ml) Amaretto

1. In a medium-size saucepan over medium heat, scald the milk. Set aside.

2. In a large bowl or food processor, combine the sugar and cornstarch. Whisk in the egg yolks and vanilla. Beat hard with a whisk or process briefly until light colored and foamy. Whisking constantly, or with the food processor running, add the hot milk gradually to the egg mixture. Pour the custard back into the saucepan.

3. Cook the sauce gently over medium-low heat, stirring constantly with a whisk, until just slightly thickened and smooth, and the sauce coats a spoon, about 5 minutes; do not boil. Pour the sauce into a storage bowl and let cool to room temperature. Refrigerate, covered, until serving time. Serve cold, pouring a little vanilla extract or Amaretto around each wedge of English Pudding.

About the Authors

Beth Hensperger is the author of more than twenty-two cookbooks, including the best-selling Not Your Mother's Slow Cooker Cookbook series, which includes *Not Your Mother's Slow Cooker Recipes for Entertaining*, *Not Your Mother's Slow Cooker Recipes Family Favorites*, and *Not Your Mother's Slow Cooker Recipes Recipes for Two*, along with the blockbuster first volume, *Not Your Mother's Slow Cooker Cookbook*. She lives in the San Francisco Bay area. Visit her website at www.bethhensperger.com and blog at www.notyourmotherscookbook.com.

Julie Kaufmann is an editor of the food section of the San José Mercury News. She is an avid home cook who has coauthored several books with Beth Hensperger. She lives in Palo Alto, California, with her husband and two children.

About the Photographer

Ellen Callaway is a professional food & product photographer. For more than twenty years, her career has spanned a diverse scope of projects from cookbooks and advertising to packaging.

Ellen also proudly created an advertising campaign to make waste diversion look fun and informative called "Recycled Beauty." In 2015, the photo series won a highly acclaimed Hatch Award. Publicity for the campaign ranged from Boston's *Chronicle* news segment to a feature article in UK's *Resource Magazine*.

In her free time, she enjoys hiking, biking, yoga, and obsessing over inconsequential details.

About the Food Stylist

Joy Howard is a food stylist and recipe developer whose work has appeared numerous cookbooks, magazines, and advertising campaigns. She writes a column on family cooking for *EatingWell* and lives in New England with her husband and daughters.

Index

Achiote paste, in Arroz con Pollo, 86
Akita Komachi rice, 28, 29
Alley, Lynn, 63
Almonds
     Brown Basmati Almondine (Julie's
       "Cheater's Pilaf"), 60
     Thai Curried Rice, 81
Amaranth, in Basic Buckwheat Groats, 111
American rice
     about, 27–28
     American Long-Grain White Rice
       recipe, 35
     rice chart, 34
Aniseed, in Bulgur and Cherry Pilaf, 117
Apple Granola, Hot, 127
Apple(s), in Sweet Brown Rice with
     Curry, Carrots, and Raisins, 61
Arborio rice, 28
     Baby Artichokes and Arborio
       Rice, 64
     Butternut Squash Risotto, 89
     Dried Mushroom Risotto, 90
     Old-Fashioned Rice Pudding, 161
     Rice Cooker Paella, 82
     Rice Pilaf with Fresh Peas, 77
     Riso, 46
     Risotto Milanese, 87
     Vegetable Paella, 84
     washing, 12
Arkansas jasmine, 26
Aroma of rice, 24
Aroma rice cookers, 8
Aromatic long-grain rice. See also Bas-
     mati rice; Jasmine rice; Texmati rice;
     Thai jasmine rice
     about, 25–26
     Moroccan Brown Rice, 57
Artichokes, in Baby Artichokes and
     Arborio Rice, 64
Asian long-grain rice, 25
Asparagus
     Asparagus and Mushroom Risot-
       to, 91
     Asparagus with Hollandaise
       Sauce, 141
     Steamed Chicken Breasts with
       Warm Mango Sauce and Coco-
       nut Rice, 154
Australia, 27
Avocado
     California Rolls, 101
     Mexican Rice and Beans, 67

Barley. See Pearled Barley, Basic
Basil leaves
     Rice with Fresh Greens for a
       Crowd, 66
     Spaghetti Squash Alfredo, 146
     Steamed Chicken Breasts on Wild
       Rice with Gingered Tomato
       Relish, 151–152
Basmati rice, 23, 25, 29
     Brown Basmati Rice, 51

Brown Rice Kheer (Indian Rice
     Pudding), 163
Carrot Basmati Pilaf, 78
Herb and Rice Dolmas, 147–149
Indian Yellow Rice, 75
Julia's Aromatic Basmatic Rice, 56
Lemon Rice, 54
One-Pot Rice and Lentils, Indian
     Style, 62
Qui's Basmati Pilaf, 73
recipe, 39
Rice with Fresh Greens for a
     Crowd, 66
Saffron Rice, 54
Steamed Chicken Breasts with
     Warm Mango Sauce and Coco-
     nut Rice, 154
Beans. See also Chickpeas
     Frijoles Negros, 138
     Italian White Beans, 140
     Mexican Rice and Beans, 87
     soaking, 137
Beer, in Arroz con Pollo, 86
Bell pepper
     Arroz con Pollo, 86
     Frijoles Negros, 138
     Mexican Rice and Beans, 67
     Rice Cooker Paella, 82
     Steamed Salmon Steaks with
       Pineapple Salsa, 155
     Vegetable Paella, 84
Berries, in Vanilla Oatmeal Crème
     Brûlée with Berries, 129
Bing cherries, in Bulgur and Cherry
     Pilaf, 117
Biryani, 25
Black beans, in Frijoles Negros, 138
Black rice
     about, 31
     Forbidden Rice recipe, 52
     Tres Lechese Rice Pudding, 162
Blend of 7 Brown Rices, 31
Boiling rice, 13
Bomba, 29
Botan rice, 42
Bouqet garn, in Brown Rice Pilaf, 74
Broccoli with Lemon Sauce, 142
Brown basmati rice
     about, 30
     Brown Basmati Almondine (Julie's
       "Cheater's Pilaf"), 60
     Brown Rice Kheer (Indian Rice
       Pudding), 163
     recipe, 51
Brown jasmine rice, 30
     Basic Buckwheat Groats, 111
     Five-Grain Pilaf, 111
     Sweet Brown Rice with Curry, Car-
       rots, and Raisins, 61
Brown rice. See also Brown basmati
     rice; Brown jasmine rice; Long-grain
     brown rice

about, 30–31
Brown Rice with Miso, 56
Germinated Brown Rice, 51
Long-or-Medium Grain Brown
     Rice, 50
rice chart, 33
Short-Grain Brown Rice, 50
Sweet Brown Rice with Curry, Car-
     rots, and Raisins, 61
Brown Rice cycle, 20
Buckwheat Groats, 110
Buddhists, 22
Bulgur and Cherry Pilaf, 117
Butternut squash
     Butternut Squash Risotto, 89
     Millet, Winter Squash, and Sweet
       Pea Pilaf, 112

Cabbage
     Steamed Chicken Breasts on Wild
       Rice with Gingered Tomato
       Relish, 151–152
     Steamed Salmon Steaks with
       Pineapple Salsa, 155
     Thanksgiving Jook, 135
Calamari, in Rice Cooker Paella, 82
Calasparra, 29
California, 27, 28. See also Carolina
     long-grain rice
California Arborio, 28
California-grown rice. See also Calrose
     rice
     brown rices, 30
     Japanese rice, 28–29
     Old-Fashioned Rice Pudding, 161
     Rice Pilaf with Fresh Peas, 77
     sweet rice, 30
California Hikari, 29
Calmati rice, 26
Calriso rice, 28
     Old-Fashioned Rice Pudding, 161
Calrose rice
     about, 22–23, 27, 28
     brown rice, 30
     sushi rice, 94
Cannellini beans, in Italian White
     Beans, 140
Capers, in Mexican Rice and Beans, 67
Cardamom pods
     Brown Rice Kheer (Indian Rice
       Pudding), 163
     Julia's Aromatic Basmatic Rice, 56
Caribbean, 23
Carnaroli rice, 28, 46. See also Risot-
     to-style rices
Carolina long-grain rice, 24, 26
     Greek Lemon and Dill Rice with
       Feta, 59
     Lemon Rice, 54
     Rice with Fresh Greens for a
       Crowd, 66
     Riz au Beurre, 73
     Saffron Rice, 54

Carrots
    Carrot Basmati Pilaf, 78
    Cauliflower with a Puree of Peas, 143
    Chirashi Sushi (Osaka Style),
        102–103
    Grated Carrots, 104
    Sweet Brown Rice with Curry, Car-
        rots, and Raisins, 61
    Thanksgiving Jook, 135
Cauliflower with a Puree of Peas, 143
Central America, 23
Champagne, Steamed Sausages and
    Sauerkraut with, 158
Chard leaves
    Steamed Chicken Breasts on Wild
        Rice with Gingered Tomato
        Relish, 151–152
    Steamed Salmon Steaks with
        Pineapple Salsa, 155
Chelo, 9
Cherries
    Bulgur and Cherry Pilaf, 117
    Maple-Cinnamon Rice Pudding, 130
    Poached Fresh Cherries, 165
    Thai Curried Rice, 81
Chicken
    Arroz con Pollo, 85
    Chicken Donburi, 70–71
    Indonesian Rice Bowl, 69
    Rice Cooker Paella, 82
    Steamed Chicken Breasts on Wild
        Rice with Gingered Tomato
        Relish, 151–152
    Steamed Chicken Breasts with
        Warm Mango Sauce and Coco-
        nut Rice, 154
Chickpeas
    Hummus, 137
    Zucchini Couscous, 107
China, 22, 25
Chinese black rice. *See* Forbidden Rice
Chinese jasmine rice, 36
Chinese-Style Plain Rice, 36
Chipotle chiles, in One-Pot Rice and
    Lentils, Indian Style, 62
Chirashi sushi, 93, 102–105
Christmas Blend rice (Lundberg), 31
Clams, in Rice Cooker Paella, 82
Cocoa, in Steamed Chocolate
    Custards, 166
Coconut milk
    Coconut Tapioca Pudding, 161
    Steamed Chicken Breasts with
        Warm Mango Sauce and Coco-
        nut Rice, 154
    Thai Curried Rice, 81
    Tres Leches Rice Pudding, 162
Confucius, 22
Converted rice, 23
    Mexican Rice, 79
    recipe, 37–38
    Rice with Fresh Greens for a
        Crowd, 66
Cook-and-reduce-heat rice cooker, 10
Cook-and-shut-off rice cookers, 9–10
Cooking with the Spices of India (Scan-
    nel), 56

Couscous
    Israeli Couscous with Orange, 108
    Zucchini Couscous, 107
Crabmeat, in California Rolls, 101
Cranberries/cranberry juice
    English Pudding with Cranberries
        and Walnuts, 169
    Maple-Cinnamon Rice Pudding, 130
    Wild Rice with Fennel and Dried
        Cranberries, 118
Crème Brûlée oatmeal, 129
Cucumber(s)
    California Rolls, 101
    Maki Sushi filling, 99
Cuisinart rice cookers, 8
Currants
    Herb and Rice Dolmas, 147–149
    Thai Curried Rice, 81
Curry paste, in Sweet Brown Rice with
    Curry, Carrots, and Raisins, 61
Custards
    Steamed Chocolate Custards, 166
    Steamed Lemon Custards, 170
Custard Sauce, English, 170

Daawat rice, 25
Dates, in Creamy Breakfast Oatmeal, 127
Della basmati rice, 39
Della Gourmet trademark, 26, 28
Della rice, 26
Deluxe electronic rice cookers, 10, 14
Dillweed
    Greek Lemon and Dill Rice with
        Feta, 59
    Steamed Sausages and Sauer-
        kraut with Champagne, 158
    Steamed Shrimp and Jasmine
        Rice, 157
Domestic Black Japonica, 31
Donburi, Chicken, 70–71
DuPont rice cookers, 8

Eggs (scrambled), for Maki Sushi, 99
Egyptian rice, 30
English Custard
    English Pudding with Cranberries
        and Walnuts, 169
    recipe, 170
Extended Keep Warm cycle, 15

Fan (rice bowl rice), 25
Farina di grano turco, 120
Farms of Texas Company, 26
Farro with Shiitakes, 109
Fennel, in Wild Rice with Fennel and
    Dried Cranberries, 118
Fennel seeds, in Bulgur and Cherry
    Pilaf, 117
Feta cheese
    Bulgur and Cherry Pilaf, 117
    Greek Lemon and Dill Rice with
        Feta, 59
Forbidden Rice, 31, 52, 162
Fowler, Lehman, 26
France, 23, 75
French Polenta, 121
French red rice, 31

Fuzzy logic rice cookers
    about, 10–11
    built-in soak cycle, 12
    face of, 14
    Reheat mode, 16

GABA cycle, 16
Germinated Brown Rice, 51
Ginger
    Brown Rice with Miso, 56
    Indonesian Rice Bowl, 69
    One-Pot Rice and Lentils, Indian
        Style, 62
    Spiced Yams with Ginger and
        Pears, 145
    Steamed Chicken Breasts on Wild
        Rice with Gingered Tomato
        Relish, 151–152
    Steamed Chicken Breasts with
        Warm Mango Sauce and Coco-
        nut Rice, 154
    Thai Curried Rice, 81
    Thanksgiving Jook, 135
Glutinous rice (sweet rice), 23, 30
Goat cheese
    French Polenta, 121
    Herb and Rice Dolmas, 147–149
Gobindavog, 29
Gomasio, 48, 50
Granola, Hot Apple, 127
Grape leaves, in Herb and Rice Dolmas,
    147–149
Grated Carrots
    Chirashi Sushi (Osaka Style),
        102–103
    recipe, 104
Greek yogurt
    Bulgur and Cherry Pilaf, 117
    Vanilla Oatmeal Crème Brûlée
        with Berries, 129
Green beans
    Rice Cooker Paella, 82
Greenmax Fine Multi Grains, 55
Greens, in Seven-Herb Rice Porridge
    (Nanakusagayu), 132–133
Grits
    Shrimp and Grits, 125
    Traditional Grits, 122

Haiga mai, 42, 162
Ham hock, in Italian White Beans, 140
Hand rolls (sushi), 93
Han giri, 94, 95
Harder setting, 15
Himalayan red rice, 31
    Basic Buckwheat Groats, 111
Hinode Brown rice, 30
Hitachi rice cookers, 8
Hollandaise Sauce, Asparagus with, 141
Homai rice, 26, 27, 30, 42
Hominy, Fresh, 123
Honen sweet rice, 30
Hummus, 137

India, 22, 25, 35, 37
Indian rice, 29
Indica. *See* Long-grain rice
Indonesia, 23, 31, 69

Induction heating, fuzzy logic rice cookers with, 11
International Rice Institute, 40
Italian parsley. *See* Parsley leaves
Italian rice, 28. *See also* Risotto-style rices
Italy, 23

Jalapeño chile
    Frijoles Negros, 138
    Mexican Rice and Beans, 67
    One-Pot Rice and Lentils, Indian Style, 62
    Steamed Salmon Steaks with Pineapple Salsa, 155
Japan, 22, 23, 27, 30
The Japanese Kitchen (Shimbo), 48
Japanese Omelet
    Chirashi Sushi (Osaka Style), 102–103
    recipe, 103
Japanese sesame seeds
    California rolls, 101
    Chicken Donburi, 70–71
    Japanese White Rice with Ume-boshi and Sesame, 45
Japanese-style rices. *See also* Calrose rice; Tamaki Gold
    about, 28–29
    Asian Multigrain Rice, 55
    Chicken Donburi, 70–71
    Seven-Herb Rice Porridge (Nanakusagayu), 132–133
    Sushi recipes, 94–101
    Thanksgiving Jook, 135
Japanese Zen Buddhists, 22
Japonica (short-grain rice). *See* Short-grain rices
Jasmati rice, 25–26
    Greek Lemon and Dill Rice with Feta, 59
    Steamed Chicken Breasts with Warm Mango Sauce and Coconut Rice, 154
Jasmine rice, 25–26. *See also* Brown jasmine rice; Thai jasmine rice
    American-grown, 25–26
    American Jasmine Rice recipe, 40
    Greek Lemon and Dill Rice with Feta, 59
    Steamed Chicken Breasts with Warm Mango Sauce and Coconut Rice, 154
    Steamed Shrimp and Jasmine Rice, 157
    Thai Curried Rice, 81
    Thai Jasmine Rice, 41

Kalijira rice, 29
Kampyo
    Chirashi Sushi (Osaka Style), 102–103
    recipe, 104
Kasha, 110
Kasmati rice, 26
Keep warm cookers, 10
Keep Warm cycle, 13, 14–15

Kitchari, 62
Kizami (shredded) *nori*, in Chirashi Sushi (Osaka Style), 102–103
Kohinoor basmati, 39
Kokuho Rose Brown Rice, 30
Kokuho Rose rice, 27, 94
Konriko, 27, 42
Korea, 22, 27
Koshi Hikari Japanese rice, 26, 28–29, 47
Krups rice cookers, 8

Lee, Ken, 23
Lemon/lemon zest
    Broccoli with Lemon Sauce, 142
    Greek Lemon and Dill Rice with Feta, 59
    Herb and Rice Dolmas, 147–149
    Lemon Rice, 54
    Moroccan Brown Rice, 57
    Steamed Lemon Custards, 170
    Tres Leches Rice Pudding, 162
Lemon Rice, 54
Lentils, in Curry, Quinoa, Lentil, and Brown Rice Pilaf, 115
Lime juice
    Arroz con Pollo, 85
    Butternut Squash Risotto, 89
    Thai Curried Rice, 81
Liu, Grace, 135
Long-grain brown rice, 30, 31
    Brown Rice Pilaf, 74
    Curry, Quinoa, Lentil, and Brown Rice Pilaf, 115
    recipe, 50
    Sweet Brown Rice with Curry, Carrots, and Raisins, 61
Long-grain rice, 22, 24–26. *See also* Basmati rice; Carolina long-grain rice; Converted rice; Jasmine rice; Texmati rice
    American Long-Grain White Rice recipe, 35
    Arroz con Pollo, 86
    Arroz Verde, 80
    Chinese-Style Plain Rice, 36
    Greek Lemon and Dill Rice with Feta, 59
    Long-or Medium-Grain Brown Rice, 50
    Mexican Rice and Beans, 67
    rice charts, 33, 34
    Rice Pilaf with Fresh Peas, 77
    Tomato-Rice Pilaf, 75
Lotus Foods, 23, 28, 29, 31, 40, 64
Louisiana popcorn rice, 26
Lowell Farms, 26, 30, 40
Lundberg
    Arborio rice, 28
    basmati rice, 39
    black rice, 31
    brown rices, 30, 51, 162
    Christmas Blend, 31
    Long-Grain Brown Rice, 30
    Wehani Rice, 52, 63

Mahatma, 24, 26, 35
Maki-su, 97
Maki sushi, 93, 97–99

Mango, in Steamed Chicken Breasts with Warm Mango Sauce and Coconut Rice, 154
McMahan, Jacquie, 79
Medium-grain rice. *See also* Arborio rice; Calrose rice; Japanese-style rices; Risotto-style rices
    about, 22–23, 27–30
    Asian Multigrain Rice, 55
    Japanese White Rice with Ume-boshi and Sesame, 45
    Long-or Medium-Grain Brown Rice recipe, 50
    Medium-Grain White Rice recipe, 42–43
    rice charts, 33, 34
Menu button, 15
Millet
    Basic Buckwheat Groats, 111
    Five-Grain Pilaf, 111
    Millet, Winter Squash, and Sweet Pea Pilaf, 112
Mint leaves
    Greek Lemon and Dill Rice with Feta, 59
    Rice with Fresh Greens for a Crowd, 66
Mirin, in Chicken Donburi, 70–71
Miso, Brown Rice with, 56
Mochi gome, 30
Multigrain blend rice, in Asian Multigrain Rice, 55
Mung dal, in One-Pot Rice and Lentils, Indian Style, 62
"Musenmai" rice, 42
Mushrooms. *See also* Shiitake mushrooms
    Asparagus and Mushroom Risotto, 91
    Dried Mushroom Risotto, 90
    Israeli Couscous with, 108
    Quinoa Mushroom Pilaf, 114

Natural Short-Grain Brown Rice, 30
New Crop Rice, 27–28, 42
Nishiki, 27, 42, 94
Nori. *See Yaki sushi nori*

Oatmeal
    Creamy Breakfast, 127
    Vanilla Oatmeal Crème Brûlée with Berries, 129
Okama (bowl), 8
Okame, 42
On/off rice cookers, 9, 14, 20
Orange zest
    Carrot Basmati Pilaf, 78
    Israeli Couscous with Orange, 108
Oryza sativa, 22
Osem Israeli couscous, 108

Pacific International, 26, 27, 30, 35
Panasonic/National rice cookers, 8
Parboiled rice. *See* Converted rice
Parboiling rice, 37
Pari rice, 25

Parmesan cheese
Baby Artichokes and Arborio Rice, 64
Butternut Squash Risotto, 89
Italian Polenta, 120
Italian Sausage Risotto, 92
Risotto Milanese, 87
Spaghetti Squash Alfredo, 146
Wehani Rice with Garden Vegetables, 63

Parsley leaves
Arroz Verde, 80
Baby Artichokes and Arborio Rice, 64
Butternut Squash Risotto, 89
Dried Mushroom Risotto, 90
Israeli Couscous with Orange, 108
Italian Sausage Risotto, 92
Japanese White Rice with Umeboshi and Sesame, 45
Lemon Rice, 54
Rice with Fresh Greens for a Crowd, 66, 667
Shrimp and Grits, 125

Peanut sauce, in Indonesian Rice Bowl, 69
Pearled Barley, Basic, 107
Pearl tapioca, in Coconut Tapioca Pudding, 161
Pears, Spiced Yams with Ginger and, 145
Peas
Arroz con Pollo, 86
Cauliflower with a Puree of Peas, 143
Chirashi Sushi (Osaka Style), 102–103
Indonesian Rice Bowl, 69
Millet, Winter Squash, and Sweet Pea Pilaf, 112
recipe, 105
Rice Cooker Paella, 82
Rice Pilaf with Fresh Peas, 77
Vegetable Paella, 84

Persian-style rice cooker, 9
Philippines, 22, 35, 75
Pickled ginger
Chirashi Sushi (Osaka Style), 102–103
Maki Sushi, 97–98

Pilafs
Bulgur and Cherry Pilaf, 117
Curry, Quinoa, Lentil, and Brown Rice Pilaf, 115
Five-Grain Pilaf, 111
indica rice for, 22
Millet, Winter Squash, and Sweet Pea Pilaf, 112
Quinoa Mushroom Pilaf, 114

Pineapple, in Steamed Salmon Steaks with Pineapple Salsa, 155
Pine nuts
Greek Lemon and Dill Rice with Feta, 59
Herb and Rice Dolmas, 147–149

Pinto beans, in Mexican Rice and Beans, 67

Polenta
French Polenta, 121
Italian Polenta, 120
Porridge cycle, 15–16, 20
Potatoes, in Steamed Sausages and Sauerkraut with Champagne, 158
Potato starch, 99
Pressure cooking, fuzzy logic rice cookers with, 11
Prevean Carnaroli, 28
Preve Family, 28
Prosciutto, in Italian White Beans, 140
Provence, France, 31
Pudding
Coconut Tapioca Pudding, 161
Old-Fashioned Rice Pudding, 161
Tres Leches Rice Pudding, 162

Queso fresco, in Mexican Rice and Beans, 67
Quick Cook cycle, 15, 20
Quinoa
Curry, Quinoa, Lentil, and Brown Rice Pilaf, 115
Five-Grain Pilaf, 111
Quinoa Mushroom Pilaf, 114

Radish sprouts, in Maki Sushi filling, 99
Raisins
Maple-Cinnamon Rice Pudding, 130
Sweet Brown Rice with Curry, Carrots, and Raisins, 61
Thai Curried Rice, 81
Red rice
about, 31
Basic Buckwheat Groats, 111
Five-Grain Pilaf, 111
Wehani Red Rice, 52
Wehani Rice with Garden Vegetables, 63

Regular cycle, 20
Regular setting, 14
Reheat mode, 16
Rhubarb and Strawberries, Poached, 165
Rice(s). See also specific types of rices
brown, 30–31
categorizing, 22–23
measuring, 17
reheating in rice cooker, 43
soaking the, 12–13
washing/rinsing, 12
Rice charts, 32–33
Rice cookers
benefits of, 7
brands, 8
cleaning your, 19
face of, 14–16
history of, 8
machine sizes, 19
steps for using, 11–13
tips for buying, 12
tips for using, 17–19
types of, 8–11
Rice Development research specialists, 27
Rice Porridge, Seven-Herb, 132–133

Rice pudding, 23
Brown Rice Kheer (Indian Rice Pudding), 163
Maple-Cinnamon Rice Pudding, 130
Old-Fashioned Rice Pudding, 161
Tres Leches Rice Pudding, 162
RiceSelect brand, 26, 28
RiceSelect Royal Blend, 26
RiceTec, Inc., 26
Richvale Red, 31
Rinsing rice, 12
Riso nero, in Tres Leches Rice Pudding, 162
Risotto con funghi secchi, 90
Risotto-style rices. See also Arborio rice
Asparagus and Mushroom Risotto, 91
Baby Artichokes and Arborio Rice, 64
Butternut Squash Risotto, 89
Dried Mushroom Risotto, 90
Italian Sausage Risotto, 92
Riso, 46
Risotto Milanese, 87
washing, 12
Riviana (Mahatma) rice, 24
Riz Parfumé, 26, 41
Riz rouge de Camargue, 31

Saffron Rice, 54
Saffron threads
Brown Rice Kheer (Indian Rice Pudding), 163
Rice Cooker Paella, 82
Risotto Milanese, 87
Saffron Rice, 54
Vegetable Paella, 84
Salmon steaks, in Steamed Salmon Steaks with Pineapple Salsa, 155
Sanyo rice cookers, 8
Sauerkraut, Steamed Sausages with, 158
Sausage
Italian Sausage Risotto, 92
Rice Cooker Paella, 82
Steamed Sausages and Sauerkraut with Champagne, 158
Scallops, in Rice Cooker Paella, 82
Scannel, Julia, 56
Seasoned Shiitake Mushrooms, 105
Seaweed wrappers. See Yaki sushi nori
Seihakumai, 42
Semisweet chocolate, in Steamed Chocolate Custards, 166
Sesame paste, in Hummus, 137
Sesame seeds. See Japanese sesame seeds
Seven-Herb Rice Porridge, 132–133
Shepherd, Renee, 69
Shiitake mushrooms
Chicken Donburi, 70–71
Farro with Shiitakes, 109
Maki Sushi filling, 99
Shimbo, Hiroko, 48
Short-grain brown rice, 30, 50

Short-grain rices. See also Arborio rice; Japanese-style rices
  about, 22–23, 27–30
  black rice as, 31
  Short-Grain White Rice recipe, 47
  Tres Leches Rice Pudding, 162
Shrimp
  Rice Cooker Paella, 82
  Shrimp and Grits, 125
  Steamed Shrimp and Jasmine Rice, 157
Snow peas
  Chirashi Sushi (Osaka Style), 102–103
  peas substituted with, 105
Soaking rice, 12–13
Softer setting, 15
South America, 35
Southeast Asia, 22, 25, 31, 69
Southern long-grain rice. See Carolina long-grain rice
Southern medium-grain rice, 28
Southern Rice Marketing, 26
South Indian red rice, 31
Spaghetti Squash Alfredo, 146
Spain, 23
Spanish rice, 29
Specialty Rice, Inc., 26
Spinach
  Arroz Verde, 80
  One-Pot Rice and Lentils, Indian Style, 62
Squash
  Butternut Squash Risotto, 89
  Millet, Winter Squash, and Sweet Pea Pilaf, 112
  Spaghetti Squash Alfredo, 146
Steamed Sticky Rice, 48–49
Steaming rice, 13, 20
Steel-cut oats, in Creamy Breakfast Oatmeal, 127
Sticky rices. See also Short-grain rices
  Steamed Sticky Rice, 48–49
  washing/rinsing, 2
Strawberries, Poached Rhubarb and, 165
Sunflower seeds, in Basic Buckwheat Groats, 110
Superfino Arborio, 28. See also Arborio rice
Sushi
  California Rolls, 101
  Chirashi Sushi (Osaka Style), 102–103
  making in a rice cooker, 94–96
  Maki Sushi, 97–99
  nigri, 93
  storing, 93
  types that Japanese home cooks make, 93
Sushi cycle, 20, 94
Sushi rice, 20, 27, 28
Sweet potatoes, in Spiced Yams with Ginger and Peas, 145
Sweet rice, 23, 30

Tahini, in Hummus, 137
Taiwan, 25, 55, 75
Tamaki Classic rice, 29, 42
Tamaki Gold, 27, 29, 47, 70, 94
Tamaki haiga mai, 162
Tamanishiki, 27
Tamari
  Chicken Donburi, 70–71
  Japanese White Rice with Umeboshi and Sesame, 45
Texas A & M University, 40
Texas Arborio rice, 26
Texmati rice, 26
  Mexican Rice, 79
  Moroccan Brown Rice, 57
  Rice with Fresh Greens for a Crowd, 66
  Riz au Beurre, 73
  Saffron Rice, 54
Thai black rice, 31
Thai jasmine rice, 22, 23, 25, 41
  Five-Grain Pilaf, 111
  Indonesian Rice Bowl, 69
  Steamed Shrimp and Jasmine Rice, 157
Thailand, 23
Thai red rice, 31
Thanksgiving Jook, 135
Tilda rice, 25, 26
Tohfa basmati, 39
Tomatoes (canned)
  Mexican Rice and Beans, 67
  Tomato-Rice Pilaf, 75
Tomatoes (fresh)
  Arroz con Pollo, 86
  Mexican Rice, 79
  One-Pot Rice and Lentils, Indian Style, 62
  Rice Cooker Paella, 82
  Steamed Chicken Breasts on Wild Rice with Gingered Tomato Relish, 151–152
  Vegetable Paella, 84
Tomato sauce/salsa, in Frijoles Negros, 138
Toshibo rice cookers, 8
Tuna (raw), for Maki Sushi filling, 99
Turkey, in Thanksgiving Jook, 135

Umeboshi plums, in Japanese White Rice with Umeboshi and Sesame, 45
Uncle Ben's rice, 24
University of California at Davis, 22–23, 27

Valencia rice
  about, 29
  Rice Cooker Paella, 82
  Vegetable Paella, 84
Vegetables (fresh or frozen). See also specific names of vegetables
  One-Pot Rice and Lentils, Indian Style, 62
  Wehani Rice with Garden Vegetables, 63

Vegetarian Dashi
  Chicken Donburi, 70–71
  Grated Carrots, 104
  Kampyo (Dried Gourd Strips), 104
  Peas, 105
  recipe, 105
  Seasoned Shiitake Mushrooms, 105
  Shiitake Mushrooms, 99
Vialone nano rice, 28, 46. See also Risotto-style rices
Vietnam, 23
Vietnamese (cargo) red rice, 31

Walnuts
  Basic Buckwheat Groats, 110
  English Pudding with Cranberries and Walnuts, 169
Wasabi
  California Rolls, 101
  Maki Sushi, 97–98
Washing rice, 12
Wehani red rice
  about, 31
  recipe, 52
  Wehani Rice with Garden Vegetables, 63
White rices. See Long-grain rice; Short-grain rices
White wine
  Dried Mushroom Risotto, 90
  Italian Sausage Risotto, 92
  Risotto Milanese, 87
  Steamed Chicken Breasts with Warm Mango Sauce and Coconut Rice, 154
  Steamed Sausages and Sauerkraut with Champagne, 158
Wild Blend, 31
Wild Pecan rice, 26, 30
Wild rice
  Steamed Chicken Breasts on Wild Rice with Gingered Tomato Relish, 151–152
  Wild Rice with Fennel and Dried Cranberries, 118
Williams Rice Milling Company, 29, 94
Williams-Sonoma, 29
Wooden bowl, for making sushi, 94

Yaki sushi nori, 97
  California Rolls, 101
  Maki Sushi, 97–99
Yams with Ginger and Pears, 145

Zojirushi rice cookers, 8
Zucchini
  Vegetable Paella, 84
  Zucchini Couscous, 107